F2
W38

Stranger Than Fiction

The Biography of Elspeth Bryce-Smith

Also by Joyce Stranger

Stranger Than Fiction

The Biography of Elspeth Bryce-Smith

Joyce Stranger

MICHAEL JOSEPH

LONDON

First published in Great Britain
by Michael Joseph Ltd
44 Bedford Square
London WC1
1984

British Library Cataloguing in Publication Data

Stranger, Joyce
   Stranger than fiction: the story of Elspeth Bryce-Smith.
   1. Bryce-Smith, Elspeth   2. Horsemanship—
   Great Britain — Biography
   I. Title
   798′.2′0924   SF309

ISBN 0 7181 2389 1

Filmset by Alacrity Phototypesetters, Weston-super-Mare.
Printed and bound in Great Britain by
Billing & Sons Limited, Worcester and London

Dedicated to the memory of Alison McInerney, daughter of Elspeth Bryce-Smith, who followed in her mother's footsteps and who, sadly, died in October 1982 whilst riding a stallion she was breaking. Alison was my friend as well as my instructor and this book is for her sisters, Tilda Manson and Jane Allen, and their children, as well as for Alison's own two daughters as a record of a very remarkable horsewoman.

I hope they will find the story as fascinating and encouraging as I do.

Joyce Stranger
November 1983

Acknowledgements

Both Elspeth Bryce-Smith and myself owe thanks to
Heather Gale. Heather took E.B.S.'s almost inde-
cipherable notes and writings, sorted them out and
typed them beautifully, so making my task very
much easier and far more enjoyable than it would
otherwise have been. Without her comprehensive
and time-consuming work this book might never
have come into being.

The basis for this story is the original diaries of Elspeth Bryce-Smith and her own accounts of her childhood and 'flapping' days. The book was written chapter by chapter from her memories and discussed in detail with her to make it as true to her life as possible. The author has been associated with E.B.S. through riding at Trefor stables, and later riding with Alison McInerney, and the memories of Elfie and her childhood and her flapping days have been a total fascination for over twenty years.

Until she retired, Elspeth Bryce-Smith was far too busy to sit and talk about the past; she was too involved in the present. In spite of illness, even on the day the final edited draft of the manuscript was discussed, 'Elfie' was out riding and did not come in until late in the evening. Horses still form an important part of her life at well over seventy years old.

All the events in this book happened over fifty years ago.

People and place names have in some cases been altered to prevent identification.

'John Graham' is, however, the real name under which Elspeth rode for over four years as a very successful jockey in flapping races.

Chapter 1

March 21st, 1913.

It was Good Friday.

The household seethed with excitement. A baby was about to be born. It was a big household; the Pollok family were upper middleclass, the kind of family known, in those days, among the more lowly inhabitants of the Lancashire village where they lived, as 'carriage folk'. Their home was a small manor house standing in large grounds, and indoor and outdoor servants were inevitable. There were now two nannies in the nursery, although at present only one baby, an enchanting little red-headed girl aged fifteen months — a fact which caused maiden aunts to purse their lips in disapproval. It was much too soon for a second child, but they would forgive both parents if it were a boy.

A son was needed to inherit the family estates in Scotland and the family rope-making business. A boy to carry on the family name. Everyone was waiting excitedly for the heir to the kingdom, and no one even dreamed of another girl being born.

The child, as was normal then, was to be born at home and the whole household seemed to be occupied, fetching and carrying, making meals, the two nannies running up and down the many stairs that led from the nurseries to the kitchen quarters.

Is the baby born yet? Surely it's a long time coming?

Even the outside staff speculated as to whether this one would be a girl or a boy, seemingly more aware than the family that Nature did not always do what was wanted.

Nanny Two was to take over the little girl; Nanny One was to be promoted and take over the heir himself, the very important child, already named Thomas.

11

Excitement spilled over when the monthly nurse in attendance announced importantly that labour had started — the child would soon be born.

The butler had prepared the celebration: whisky in a crystal decanter, champagne for the doctor and the family, port for the staff to wet the baby's head. The tray was set with gleaming glassware for all the household. Even the kitchen and outdoor staff would join in this celebration. The tray, waiting to be taken upstairs, was a constant reminder of the event now taking place.

'When little Thomas was born . . . ' 'Little Mr Thomas . . .' 'A son for Sir. Wouldn't Sir be thrilled?' Girls in those days were very much inferior citizens, without a vote, their property belonging to their husbands, their rights almost unrecognised, the jobs and careers open to them, especially in a family like this, very few indeed.

Both nannies, the maids and the butler were frantically going through the many tasks that were essential in a well-run household: coals to carry, water to boil, clothes to wash in dolly tubs, with scrubbing boards, ironing, nothing conveniently arranged, with so many stairs to climb that by the end of the day the indoor servants had covered many miles and were worn out. They rose at dawn and worked until bedtime. Nobody thought of limiting their hours.

In the nursery Nanny One ruled her nursery maids and the children with rigid discipline. In the kitchen Cook was supreme. The butler was a personality in his own right, looked up to with awe, almost as important as Sir himself.

Time went on and, alarmingly, no announcement was made. Childbirth was a dangerous affair and everyone worried. Cook, a martinet for meals on time, grumbled to herself bad-temperedly because dinner was served late and her beautifully prepared meal was dried up and spoiled. No one seemed to have their minds on eating.

At last the doctor came down the stairs and made his announcement. He was not happy as the baby was not a vigorous child, like its little sister.

'A little girl.'

Not the longed-for son. Not exactly a disaster, but a particularly acid maiden aunt told the second daughter many years afterwards that she must have been 'a careless mistake, to say the very least'! The small gap between the children became a matter for family comment long after it had ceased to matter to the parents at all. A child had been born.

The new baby, fortunately, was unaware of the disappointment, of the champagne being returned to the cellar and the doctor rewarded with very mundane port. What was worse, she was a very sickly baby and for some hours it seemed not only that there would be no son, but no child at all. An agitated nurse, contemplating the terrible possibility of a dead, unchristened baby denied her chance in Heaven by being buried in unconsecrated ground, sent for the minister. Without consulting anyone as the mother was too ill and the father unavailable, she had the child christened Mary, a fact that when discovered caused considerable annoyance.

This child was to remain, all her life, totally unpredictable and able to baffle everybody by her inability to do what was expected of a young lady of her station, or even what was expected of a baby. She was a girl when she should have been a boy; she was expected to die but proved possessed of a remarkable hardiness as she recovered, over and over again, both as a child and an adult, when she was not expected to live.

Her mother had her re-christened Elspeth — 'a gift of God'. Was God careless too, Elspeth asked the ever-critical and vinegary aunt many years later, but her aunt had no answer. The Lord moved in mysterious ways, and didn't always perform wonders.

Her babyhood was uneventful. She was a beautiful baby with thick black hair, blue eyes and pink cheeks. The starchy nannies relaxed at times to compliment and comfort her, and often when she was older to tell her how lovely she had been. They were not tactful women and seldom thought of the effects of their words on a tiny child not yet blessed with

13

adult understanding. One of their favourite sayings as they finished the saga of the lovely baby was to add, with a sigh and a heaving of immense bosoms, something that was to prove a provoking reminder to her for years afterwards: 'Ah well. Beautiful in the cradle, ugly at the table.'

Almost no one of those around her ever stopped to consider how the children felt; and particularly this child who was fated to be the member of the family struck down by one of the most dreaded of all childhood illnesses, when she was only four years old.

Before she reached that age the longed-for Thomas had really arrived and Nanny One was now nurse to the heir to the family, promoted and very busy indeed with the baby boy. Meanwhile, disaster overtook the little girl.

She developed poliomyelitis, which was then known as wasting sickness. She was desperately ill. Once more she defeated all the prophets of doom and recovered, but she lost her bonny appearance and became a very small child, with a wistful appearance, soft flyaway mouse-coloured hair, and a peaky face with enormous eyes and an expression that reminded everyone of an elf, and earned her the nickname Elfie. The name remained to plague her all her life.

Nursery life was regimented. Parents lived their own lives and the children, washed and clean and beautifully dressed, came to visit them when requested. Her illness changed some of this routine for Elfie, but she did not then understand that she was an unusual child, seeing far more of her parents than the healthy members of the family.

The days were long, punctuated by the meals brought by an overworked nursery maid who spent her life running up and down stairs with trays of food and trays of dirty crockery, with tea for the two nannies, with milk, with cocoa, for the children. As a great privilege she was allowed to help with ironing the elaborate clothes that everyone wore.

The flatirons had to be heated carefully, not too hot to scorch but hot enough to produce a perfection rarely seen today. The ironing was very important indeed and no

14

under-maid could ever do it without Nanny's highly critical eye on her to ensure that the children were always perfectly turned out, as befitted a properly run nursery. A single crease and Nanny's reputation would suffer.

The children had to behave, to mind their Ps and Qs, to be polite, nannies did not allow tantrums and tempers. Elfie, a passionate child with an enquiring mind that thought for itself and did not conform to the family beliefs, had problems with her elders. They were not eased by her discovery when at last she was well enough to want to venture out of bed, that she had legs that did not work and that, it was thought, would never work again.

She had been a very active child with a delight in movement, with a passionate desire to explore, to find out what was outside in the big wide world that hid itself beyond the immense gardens. She always wanted to know; she hated the Victorian habit of answering questions with 'Because' or 'Do as you are told'.

'Why?' 'Because I say so, Miss.' She wanted to know why. Why was she a careless mistake? Why was she a girl when she ought to have been a boy?

She was a cripple. Why? Why did God let it happen? She was different: she couldn't run with the other children or play with them; she was confined to an existence bounded by bed, by chair, and by a basket wheelchair that she hated, especially as when her mother wheeled her out the village women spoke across her as if she were daft and not just unable, at that moment, to walk. The stupid women behaved as if she would never walk again. She would walk. She would walk. She would, she would, she would.

She declared it to herself, passionately, over and over again. It was a thought to buoy her up through hours of loneliness and sometimes of misery, though she had a happy nature that overcame despair. She was ugly, both nannies said so, although not in so many words but it stuck in her mind for all her life. Her sister was a beauty, her brother Thomas sturdy and handsome and William, who soon also made his way into the world, his advent approved of by the

15

critical maiden aunts because he was male, also thrived. The other children ran and played and went on mysterious journeys that couldn't be shared by a helpless chairbound small girl. There was neither radio nor television to while away long hours spent on her own as all the adults were busy.

Nanny, her mother, and later a governess, would make sure she had fresh air and a change of scene. She was dressed warmly and a rug put over the useless legs that she so hated. Thin legs, white legs, legs that refused to work, ending in feet so small she hated them even more than her legs because she was sure they would never grow and bear her weight. Wasted legs.

On these ventures into the world her mother insisted also on a cloche hat on her head with a veil to protect her from sun and wind. Only five years old, feeling a freak, dressed like a freak as no other child wore a veil, she was sure it was because she was too ugly for people to see. This conviction grew as the women asked if she could dress herself, if she could feed herself, if she had to be, you know, or could she do it by herself. She began to feel like an alien being, and railed against their stupidity, wishing they would talk to her as if she were there and not some strange creature unaware of her surroundings, pushed out, a body that had no reality for anyone but herself.

'Such a burden on the family. Poor things, to be saddled with a child like that,' the women said, in her hearing, as if she were deaf and dumb and blind as well as daft.

Great Britain was at war but it did not affect the children, and since their father was in a reserved occupation he remained at home. They were far too young to understand the pressures on the adults. The reserved occupation was a considerable advantage for Elfie, as in spite of a busy life her father determined to help her overcome her disability. They developed a relationship that was closer than that between most fathers and their children.

'Why can't I walk?' became her despairing cry as the other children went off on exciting expeditions and she was left alone with a succession of governesses — unimaginative women who taught by rote and had little sympathy. Tom Pollok recognised the outstanding qualities in his little daughter. The women of the household, including her mother and the many visiting aunts, answered her in varying ways, but with the same words and in tones that made it hard for her to believe them. 'Be patient, you'll get better in time. Just do your exercises and work hard. You are very lucky, you have so many toys and books.'

Toys didn't make up for legs that refused to work; for being captive in the house and unable to run in the fields or explore; and this was a child who needed to explore, who needed wide horizons, who needed to grow and stretch her imagination and to expand her ideas. She became more and more frustrated as no one seemed able to talk to her, to listen to her, to help her channel her riotous imagination.

Her father understood, so that she became passionately attached to him, longing for the hours he spent with her, for their long conversations that roved the world. When she asked why she couldn't walk he always had an answer that comforted her: 'You're special; you're different,' as if being different was a virtue and not a vice.

Elfie adored him. He liked spending time with her; it wasn't a duty. He didn't treat her like a baby, as everyone else seemed to.

He knew that she would not be fobbed off with platitudes. She had to be helped to find herself, to find ways of escaping from her prison of disability and to be as whole as any child could be; perhaps to prepare her for an adult life that held no further opportunity for her than that to be found in her own mind.

Nobody seemed to think she would ever walk again. It certainly seemed a very forlorn hope looking at the wasted legs and tiny feet that she covered whenever she could, only too painfully aware of them and sure they were hideous to other people.

She might never again know what it was to walk; but her father was determined that although her body might be crippled, her mind would never be stunted, and that she would not be allowed to lapse into bitterness or envy as he would show her a way to freedom that many whole people never knew.

Chapter 2

Most children are too busy to notice much of their surroundings. Active, adventurous, exploring, always racing from one event to another, in afteryears the childhood home is often only a dim memory. Elfie, penalised by her inability to join in games, lay helpless and had time to grow to love Acrefield, the big house to which the family had moved from The Mill.

She loved the rambling corridors, down which she was so often carried; the staircases and passageways; and the high moulded ceilings, at which she so often stared. She spent her time flat on her back, and it gave her a very different viewpoint to that of the rest of the world.

There were always a lot of servants. The house was full of people, yet they were all so busy, as every room had to be kept immaculate. There had to be a governess for Elfie's benefit as she must not grow up illiterate, but to Elfie the women who filled such positions seemed always to be ogresses.

The worst of them was Miss Pierce, with her witch's nose and chin, her small angry hot little eyes, her readiness to take offence and to impress on the children that she was a personage in her own right. A lady, stooping to help educate them, doing Elfie's mother a favour as Miss Pierce was not a working woman.

'You do not do that. It is not proper.'

'Nice children do not behave like that.'

'I expect seemly behaviour from all of you. I have never seen such behaviour.'

'That is not "refained".' (Being 'unrefained' was almost the worst crime any child or adult could commit in Miss Pierce's eyes.)

19

Elfie was constantly exposed to conflicting worlds. Miss Pierce was possessed of an inordinate sense of convention and propriety. The child was her chief victim, hating her the more because she was very sensitive and imaginative and vulnerable.

Elfie loved to lie in the garden, on a camp bed that was put in a small flagged square at the bottom of a flight of oval steps that led from the open French windows of the drawing room, and allowed her to look out at the garden where Tom Tomlinson was supreme ruler.

He was an autocrat. The family found him funny and laughed at him behind his back — and nicknamed him Tom Tom. He was aided by a lanky fourteen-year-old, tow-headed, freckled and with a happy laugh, named Eddie.

Elfie was put out alone on the patio, a huge umbrella shading her from the sun, a luxurious rug folded back to expose her legs to the air, and hopefully strengthen them. She was aware of adults who came to look at her; she saw more of adults than do most children. They came to make sure she was safe, warm enough, or not too warm, that the sun wasn't shining in her eyes. Elfie, unduly conscious of those strange legs exposed to everyone's gaze, was sure they came to look at her legs, to look at the freak, and having looked went away to titter about her among themselves.

The gardener and the boy were aware of the child, lying there, watching them, eagerly greeting the spaniels when they came to sniff at her, to lick at her hand, to lie briefly out of the sun in the shade, panting, and then race off again, able to move and run and see what lay behind the big hawthorn tree as she never could.

Tomlinson came to talk to her, to rest briefly, to smile and tell her of his own daughter, Nell, a few years older than Elfie, who was really crippled. Miss Elsie (he never used the family name for her) might walk one day, almost certainly would walk. But Nell never would.

Tomlinson never hurt her feelings by tactless remarks. He told her what Nell had been doing; he talked of the flowers, and told her little stories about the outside world.

'I've been talking to Tom Tom,' she told Miss Pierce one day when the governess came to fetch her.

'You are a very naughty girl. How dare you speak to him like that. Tom Tom is not a proper name to use. It is very rude indeed. I'm ashamed of you, Miss.'

'It's Miss Elsie's special name for me,' Tomlinson said, with considerable dignity. He felt that the governess was being unnecessarily severe with the little girl. 'I like it.'

Eddie, not far away, turned his back to hide his grin. He had his own name for Miss Pierce and it wasn't a polite name either. But he was wise enough never to tell it to the child.

After that Tom Tom often broke off his work, though very briefly, to talk to the child. Lonely for other children, Nell became an imaginary friend, a girl with whom she could hold long conversations, a girl who understood what it was like to be always dependent on others, forced to listen to those who held you captive. Only her father was always welcome, and the two outside men (Eddie, nine years older than she, seemed very grown up). None of them ever made her feel a nuisance or a burden or a freak.

Tomlinson joined in her pretend conversations with Nell, and would come and ask if Nell had been to visit today. Nanny was angry: as if it wasn't bad enough having a charge who was chair- or bedbound without her talking to herself like an addlepated halfwit.

Nanny often made her feel like a daftie who ought perhaps to be locked up. She didn't mean to, but she set strange standards that seemed odd to this child, who had too much time to observe adult vagaries.

Miss Pierce convinced her that she was rude, badly behaved and wicked. This feeling grew out of all proportion because somehow they always managed to put her bed under some bush or tree that dropped giant spiders on her. She was terrified of spiders; she was helpless, unable to move and they crawled across her, or marched, on long thin hairy legs, determinedly towards her face. She had nightmares about them and visions of them growing bigger and bigger, stinging her, perhaps to death.

21

She screamed.

Miss Pierce, advancing on her almost like a giant spider herself, angry at being called out yet again by this wretched child, removed the creature and glared at her.

'I never heard such a fuss about nothing. A thoroughly unseemly scene.'

Somehow Tomlinson and Eddie always seemed to be busy in another part of the garden when the spiders dropped.

Miss Pierce went and Elfie mimicked her to herself: 'Behave yourself, Elspeth. I am ashamed of you. You are a thoroughly unseemly child.' She made a face at Miss Pierce's retreating back, and later, in the nursery, she amused herself by drawing caricatures of the governess which she had to keep well-hidden.

The governess was almost chinless, with a thick-lipped angry mouth, a large nose, hair piled on top of her head in a bun and steel-rimmed spectacles and was easy to caricature. Her expression was daunting.

Elfie loved summer. The sounds of haymaking in the fields beyond the garden; the clatter of a pony and trap passing the house; the dreamy feeling of the hot days; and the brilliant flowers that sometimes Tom Tom picked and brought to her, a tiny nosegay of her own, special, a present from him to her. A real present because she knew that her parents were only tolerated in the garden; the flowers belonged to Tomlinson — even her mother knew that. Her mother who never asked anyone permission to do anything. Her mother, always so busy, and beautiful. Sometimes in her riding clothes, hurrying out to ride side-saddle for long hours. To ride! Or coming briefly to kiss the child goodbye as she set off to some committee meeting, driving herself in the pony trap. She was one of the best women drivers in the country.

Left behind, Elfie dreamed of riding and driving, of a horse of her own.

Chapter 3

The other children, as a special treat, were taken to see the Shire horses in the stables at their father's rope factory in Liverpool. They came home full of the tale. Elfie envied them very little, but she did envy them that. She wanted to see the Shire horses so desperately.

She turned to her books and looked at the pictures of them. Great heavy horses with huge heads and beautiful wise eyes, flowing manes and tails and the wonderful feathering round their giant hooves. Little foals with odd gangly bodies and hooves far too big for their legs.

She wanted to go too.

The stables were in Lodge Lane (even that sounded romantic). Other manufacturers were beginning to have motor lorries, but Elfie's father loved his horses and knew his men loved them too. They spent hours with them, grooming them, cleaning up, turning them out as the best turnouts in Liverpool, driving them proudly along the cobbled streets, holding up the smelly motor lorries with their noisy engines, dressing them in their garlands and brasses with tiny brightly coloured flags in their plaited manes and with tails twisted with bright ribbons for the Mayday parades.

There was still a forge in every village and the village blacksmith was busy from early morning until late at night. There were still the stallion men who toured their stallions from one farm to another. They were usually such tiny men it was difficult to understand how they could manage the huge beasts. There were still high entries of Shire horses at the country fairs and the agricultural shows; still the clatter of hooves from almost every tradesman's cart.

Elfie lay and listened, and longed more and more to go and see for herself. One Sunday, when the other children went and she stayed at home, she refused to be comforted. It wasn't fair. She wanted to see the big horses. She sobbed for hours, almost making herself ill, alarming Nanny and being chided without any sympathy at all by Miss Pierce who couldn't understand why anyone should even want to see a horse.

Ellen, the nursery maid who of all the household perhaps understood best, tried to comfort her. She could draw, and the others couldn't. Look at this lovely picture she drew yesterday. It was a picture of a horse and that didn't help at all.

She had all these wonderful books her father had bought her; but the book that Ellen picked up was a picture book of British ponies.

She had these lovely dolls her mother dressed for her. Look at the fine needlework and think of all the hours she spent just for you and just look at the lovely lace on the underwear and the velvet cloak. She didn't want dolls. She wanted to go to Liverpool with the other children and see the horses.

'Oh, come on, Miss Elfie, just dry your eyes and Ellen'll make you something lovely for tea. What would you like, love?'

She didn't want any tea. She wanted her father to come home and take her to Liverpool to see the horses.

She had cried herself to sleep by the time he did come up to see her that night. He looked down at her. He listened to Nanny and heard Miss Pierce's tale of the dreadful, ridiculous, unseemly carrying on, and made his own plans.

Elfie was taken in her bathchair to Liverpool by taxi. She couldn't believe any of it. She sat in her chair on the ferry across the Mersey, staring at the buildings, at the water, at the people around her. And then there was another taxi drive to the stables and the ropeworks, where she was wheeled among women in shawls who smiled at her. They were in charge of the clattering and clanking machines that twisted more different sizes of rope than she had

24

believed could exist. The smell of it excited her. It was all so different.

Her father laughed and joked with the women, teasing them. He knew their names and the names of their husbands and children. He looked at the samples of work they were doing and examined the machines. He talked to the men, who obviously thought him a very good employer and would do anything for him. Everyone came to talk to Elfie, not as if she were an odd little cripple and a freak, nor a burden, nor an unseemly nuisance always doing or saying the wrong thing, but just like they would talk to their own children. And sitting in her chair because she chose to, and couldn't be bothered at that moment to stand up and walk about.

And then they went down to the stables.

It was a weekday, and not a Sunday which was the day that the other children visited. It was a workday, the horses were out on their rounds, the men very busy and mostly there were only names above empty stalls. But there was the stable smell that she would never forget as long as she lived, the smell of clean straw and the breathtaking smell of the horses (some of the Shires were in, resting).

The men were so proud of their horses and their harness. Hides gleamed, manes were silken, combed frequently, and so were tails. The feathering round the great hooves was cleaned with bran. Elfie was shown the harness, the leather burnished till it shone; the polished brasses; and the show gear. She was shown the horses: most of them were black with white feathery legs. She gave one a carrot, felt the soft lips against her hand, the velvet touch of the muzzle dipped to take the goody from her, savoured the hayladen breath.

As she watched and smelled and listened to the rhythm of their breathing, the rustle of hooves in the straw, the clank and clatter as the men worked, she knew why her father loved horses.

She wanted to take them and hold them and treasure them; she wanted to be with them, to care for them, to ride

25

them. Ned, the Head Groom, watching the child's face, stepped forward and lifted her out of her chair and high into the air, so that she sat astride a beautiful black mare named Nancy. He put a strap round the mare's neck for the child to hold and told her to pretend she was riding.

With her imagination, there was no pretence. She was away, galloping over sands, riding up dunes, away to the moon and back. Her excitement was so intense that she was unaware of the faces watching her, looking at ecstacy. To men who loves horses, she belonged among them: they did not need to be told how she felt.

Later that day she told her father she and Nancy had galloped up in the clouds.

'No,' he said thoughtfully. 'You didn't gallop. The clouds wouldn't let you. You did a lovely slow canter.'

A slow canter. Of course she had. He was absolutely right.

She did not want to get down. She had fallen in love, with a dream, with a hope, with a burning desire to be with horses, to live with horses, to work with horses.

It was time to go. She was lifted down, put into the hated chair, and given plaits of Nancy's mane and tail to take home.

Once home she could talk of nothing else. Miss Pierce thought the expedition most ill-advised, putting ideas into the child's head, absurd ideas. As if she could ever live with horses and work with horses.

To Elfie, the visit had been pure heaven. Her father took her with him more and more often, realising how much time she spent alone. Sometimes he took her on weekdays, but most wonderful of all were the Sundays when the horses were all in and the men were busy cleaning the tack, feeding, mucking out and grooming. It was an escape for both father and daughter.

Horses occupied her daydreams and her midnight dreams. She talked about them endlessly. She kept Nancy's plaits as a talisman, and when people annoyed her more than usual she left their boring company and hid herself in the

world of her mind, galloping endless miles, to a place where
stable talk was the only talk and the great Shires came to
greet her. In her dreams she leaped without help on to a
hunter as big as Nancy and cantered off across the hills.

Chapter 4

The passion for horses grew. It helped to keep her from despair; her legs hurt so much.

Her life was never comfortable. She knew everyone was trying to help but the doctors had fitted her with metal splints that made her more miserable than ever. The calipers were heavy and she was often in pain. Her mother and Nanny were determined she would walk; try and walk; try. She did try, constantly, but her legs had ideas of their own, and would not obey her commands. Frustration grew.

It was not helped by her governess's lack of understanding. She grew to hate Miss Pierce and wished she would go. The governess did not even obey her own rules.

One very hot day Elfie had been put to lie on her camp bed on the little flagged court. She was dreamy, an umbrella shading her from the sun, her legs exposed to the air to strengthen them — a hope that seemed to her rather odd, but there was nothing she could do about it. Mother knew best, as she was so often told. If Mother didn't, Nanny did. And, of course, Miss Pierce knew everything — though she knew very little about horses and couldn't tell a Shire from a Haflinger.

The garden was brilliant with flowers and Eddie and Tom Tom were working out of sight. Somewhere bees were swarming. Then suddenly Elfie realised she was covered in bees. She detested spiders, but the bees were pretty with their furry bodies. They crawled over her, and she watched them dreamily. Perhaps they thought she was a flower and they would find honey. It was an entertaining thought; she must smell very nice, even if her legs looked horrible. But they didn't mind her legs, they crawled on those too.

Miss Pierce, coming out to see that her charge was safe

and not too hot, or blinded by the sun in her eyes, saw the
bees and screamed.

Half the household came running. The noise was incredible. Elfie grinned to herself. They were being most
unseemly. They were frantic; they argued; their voices
grew shriller and shriller.

'She'll be stung to death, poor lamb.' Which was not a
reassuring thought and extremely unhelpful. But then grown
ups were like that, seeing death and disaster and improper
behaviour round every corner.

She mustn't move.

As if she could move.

What shall we do?

Very gently, wondering why she had to be seemly when
adults could be so unseemly, she picked off the bees, one by
one, until none were left.

'They've gone now,' she said.

Peace was restored, and she was shifted to lie under the
huge may tree, which she much preferred as the next spring
she could catch the blossom drifting down and examine the
tiny petals. She examined them with the artist's eye she was
beginning to develop.

She often wondered why anyone should think that bees
only came to the flagged terrace. Didn't people realise that
they could actually fly, and visited all honey-bearing
flowers? She was still surrounded by flowers; even more
flowers when the may tree was in bloom. It was one more
mystery to ponder among the many mysteries that the adult
world produced for her. All her life she remained very
attached to bees, and they often settled on her, but never
stung her.

Her wish to be rid of Miss Pierce was to come true a few
months later, through Tom Tom and Eddie.

Lying in the garden, watching the men, Elfie dreamed of
walking.

When you walk.

The words became a talisman, a phrase to be hoarded and
repeated; a recurrent theme; a hope for a future when she

would be the same as other people, and her tiny feet would have grown. Tom Tom, bent and thin and grim-faced, with his straggly grey beard and corduroy trousers tied below the knee with string, looked at her legs as if they were just normal legs. But she had to test him.

One day when he brought her flowers, which he often did, picking some also to take home to Nell, Elfie asked if Nell's legs were like hers. He looked at them for a moment and then said 'They're straight, and they'll grow.' He dismissed them, unimportant parts of her. They weren't what mattered. Tom Tom was always so easy to understand, unlike many of the other adults around her. He knew what was important and what was not, and her mind was important; how she thought and what she thought about, not her legs.

She tested Eddie too, as he came up to her one day, much more slowly than usual, and she thought he was looking at her legs, suddenly noticing them for what they were. Up to then they had been covered. Eddie was always very shy with her, although he came and spoke to her. She was Miss Elsie, the daughter of the people in the lovely house where he worked; they were gentry, and he was just the gardener's boy.

Elfie, obsessed by her ugliness, her difference, her horrible useless legs, watched him coming, sure he was disgusted by her, not realising that he had brought a gift for her. He didn't even notice her legs. He felt he was being overbold, perhaps would be rejected. But he wanted very badly to give her his present. Both were unaware that this tiny offering was going to make a difference in Elfie's life, and also make her more bewildered than ever by the extra-ordinary attitudes sometimes taken up by adults.

Puzzled, she watched Eddie approach. He must loathe the sight of her to come so slowly, as if he had to nerve himself to look at her. He stood by the bed.

He was carrying a pot full of growing violets. Elfie saw how beautiful they were. She loved them. She could take them up and have them by her bed; she could paint them. She would treasure them, if they really were for her. And then a horrible thought struck her: perhaps they were for Nell and he had brought them to show her. Elfie wouldn't begrudge Nell the violets, but she really hoped, desperately, that they were for her.

'They're for you, Miss Elsie,' Eddie said. 'I growed them at home, special. They knows I've brought them and said you could have them.'

Elfie was enchanted; she wanted to hold them to her. Eddie put them, very carefully in order not to damage any of the fragile stems, on the stool by her bed.

She didn't know how to voice her delight and her words sounded so inadequate, out of all proportion to the pleasure he was giving her. No one had ever thought of anything so likely to exchant her.

'Thank you, Eddie. I've never had anything grown for me before,' she said. He had made her feel very special.

He was so pleased that he began to chatter to her, talking of everything and anything. But Elfie's mind was still on her major disadvantage: she was quite sure he must find her disgusting and was only trying to be kind. Nobody ever seemed to think of her as someone normal; she was that odd child with the funny legs.

Eddie was aware of her distraction.

'What's bothering you, Miss Elsie?' he asked.

She had never told anyone else exactly how she felt; they would have told her not to be silly but she would have been sure they were only saying it, making her feel better, not meaning it at all. Eddie seemed somehow to be able to understand.

She told him how she felt lying there, her legs exposed to everyone's gaze instead of being covered-up. He looked at her in astonishment. He hadn't even noticed her legs. He looked at them now.

'Bit skinny, maybe,' he said. 'But them's only legs. I was looking at your eyes; you've got better, nicer eyes than anyone I ever met. And anyway, think of them soldiers down the road, at the home, back from the war. Some's only got one leg and crutches; some's got no legs at all.'

31

'I wouldn't mind one leg and crutches if I could walk,' Elfie whispered.

'That's daft.' Faced with a child that felt at such a disadvantage, Eddie could cope. His voice was robust.

'You've got two legs and two arms. And two eyes. Allus eat everything you can eat and drink and them legs'll grow. Flowers need water, remember or they don't grow; and you're like these violets. I've fed and watered them real well. They was proper weedy when I potted them. Never think they'd come at all, but they have. You're like them, and as pretty as them too. You just never give up, Miss Elsie, you live and never be afraid of what the Lord's given you; let people see. You've more than most. There's some as can't see and some as can't talk, and some can't tell one flower more than another. I guess you're more real than any of 'em.'

Tom Tom called him. They might see him from the house and he was wasting time. Their time that they paid for. Eddie smiled and went away and that was the last time Elfie thought too much about her legs.

She had lovely eyes, he'd said. And Eddie and Tom Tom didn't think she was strange. And she knew they said what they thought and would have told her outright if she were. They didn't try to reassure her with words that she did not always believe. It was easy to tell from people's eyes whether they meant what they said or not.

She lay looking at the violets. They were so dainty; so beautifully shaped, so delicately marked. She touched them, very gently, aware of the texture of the petals and the tough yet tiny stems. They had been weedy like her and now they were sturdy for their kind, and growing beautifully. They were perfect and so would she be, she was sure.

It began to rain. Nobody remembered she was outside.

Then the French windows were opened and Nanny raced out, picked up Elfie and rushed in with her, guiltily aware that she should have been watching. The child was soaked.

Rain had poured suddenly from the sky, almost without warning. Elfie was dried and dressed in her nightclothes, her wet clothes taken away.

Tom Tom brought in the bed and Eddie the stool. It began to thunder; the rain lashed down. Lightning scorched across the sky. Outside were Tom Tom's flowers and the beautiful violets, all getting ruined by the heavy storm. Her precious gift was being battered and broken and drowned. She lay helpless, and yelled for someone to bring them in.

The storm was frightening. Eddie ran to fetch the flowers and Miss Pierce arrived to see what on earth all the commotion was about. Eddie ran back into the room. He was dirty, he was soaked, but he had saved the picked flowers and the little pot of violets and he stood there grinning with pleasure, knowing he had done well.

Elfie was wearing a beautifully made nightie: starched, ironed, be-ribboned and clean. She hugged the flowers against her; muddy flowers, soaking wet, and the nightdress was marked and dirty.

Miss Pierce, already annoyed by the sight of the thin, dirty, bedraggled gardener's boy standing on the clean carpet, and by the din of the storm, was infuriated to such an extent that she knocked the plants flying, shouting at the child. Violets, earth and broken pot fell on to the pearl-grey carpet and chipped one of the four fluted pillars in the room, just beside the couch on which Elfie lay.

Elfie screamed and began to cry. Her lovely flowers were ruined and Eddie had gone to such trouble for her and they were just like her; they had been weedy and had grown as she would grow. Now they would die. Her misery was out of all proportion to the event as far as the governess could see. Wretched child. Stupid boy.

Elfie's howls grew to such a pitch that they brought other people running. Tom Tom and Eddie began to collect the bits of plant pot and tried to rescue the flowers; Ellen, the housemaid, came in, took an appalled glance at the scene, rushed for dustpan and brush; and Elfie's mother came into the room.

'What on earth is going on?' she asked, in a voice that should have warned the governess.

'He,' Miss Pierce said, pointing to Eddie, 'had the audacity to give the child flowers in a *pot*.' The pot might have been the ultimate obscenity judging by her tone, and Elfie stopped crying, hoping her mother might take her part in this totally baffling scene. Her mother was watching the governess, an unusual expression on her face, but Miss Pierce was not observant and went on, 'I won't have the child consorting in this intimate fashion with common garden boys. It's degrading and disgusting.'

That was too much for Eddie.

'Bluidy bitch—' he said.

It was a lovely expression and absolutely right.

Elfie, distraught at the loss of her lovely flowers and the spoiling of a perfect day, echoed it, in more refined accents and with a great deal more venom in her voice than there had been in Eddie's.

Miss Pierce, losing her temper completely, smashed her hand across Elfie's face. As Elfie began to bawl again she raised her voice to the gardeners.

'Get out. Get out, you filthy gardeners.'

As they turned to go, Nanny came into the room, breathing fast as she had hurried, having been fetched by Ellen who had been shocked by what she called the 'goings-on'.

Nanny stopped Tom Tom and Eddie leaving and explained that she had given Eddie permission go give the violets, which he had grown especially, as a gift.

'See to Elfie, will you please, Nanny. Thank you Eddie and Tomlinson for your help and for your gifts. Go and ask them to give you some warm drinks in the kitchen; you're both soaked through. Miss Pierce, I would like a word with you in the morning-room.'

Elfie watched her mother lead the way, with quiet dignity, from the room.

Nanny, who had had too many set-tos with Miss Pierce, comforted her forlorn charge and took the plant down to Tomlinson to be repotted. Later that day it was put on the windowsill and the cut flowers were carefully arranged in a vase by the bed.

Bedtime brought mother and kisses and cuddles, but also

34

an explanation as to why no nice little girl could ever say anything as dreadful as 'Bluidy bitch'. Elfie thoroughly deserved her smack, but as Miss Pierce left that evening and none of the children saw her again, she did sometimes wonder if perhaps Miss Pierce had not been the most reliable of adults. At times she had certainly appeared more unseemly than the children she was supposed to teach.

'I'm glad she's gone,' Elfie said, when Nanny came to tuck her up.

Nanny, too, might have detested the governess but she knew what was right.

'Just remember her in your prayers, like a nice girl,' she said, as she left the room.

Elfie had to say her prayers lying on her back, not kneeling by her bed like the other children. They had come to see her, elated at the thought of no more Miss Pierce which meant going away to school. But that was going to make Elfie lonelier than ever, as at least they had been there after tea, although she did not see much of them; they had their own affairs.

Elfie lay in bed, thinking. It had been a very hard smack indeed and her face was bruised and hurt. Her feelings had also been hurt as she had heard Miss Pierce making venomous remarks about spoiled cripples and legs. She was upset about Tom Tom and Eddie and bewildered by the governess's treatment of them. She could not for the life of her see how they could be degrading, which she knew was a very horrible word.

She must never lie, above all she must not lie to God, so her prayer took a great deal of consideration. At last she decided on the right words. She might hate Miss Pierce and Miss Pierce obviously hated her, but she would do her best. Be charitable, Nanny had said. She decided to be charitable, although she thought that meant giving to the poor — who her mother said were always with us. The household had a stock of such odd sayings.

She asked God to bless everyone she loved, which included Tom Tom and Eddie, and then added her postscript.

35

'Please, God, don't make any more Miss Pierces. She's not a nice person and surely one is enough. For Christ's sake, amen.'

Next day, according to all the household, the storm had cleared the air. So had Miss Pierce's departure, and the garden was bright and sunny and there was no fear whatever that such a terrifying scene would recur. It was blissful under the trees, the lawn mower acting as a lullaby, birds, bees and butterflies flying among the shrubs, and flowers around her.

But she wouldn't have the rug off her legs. As far as she could see they had caused all the trouble and, even with Eddie's words to comfort her, the thought that her peculiarity had brought such trouble on everyone bothered her.

Saddest of all, her father had been the only person the day before not to come near her. He always came to say goodnight and she was sure he was saddened by the thought of his small daughter using such dreadful language. This was his ultimate punishment. There could be no other reason.

She was so unhappy at the thought of his displeasure that she begged for him to come the night after Miss Pierce left. He came, saddened and solemn, and realising her misunderstanding told her he had drunk far too much the night before and he was a disgrace to the family. She began to cry, saying she loved him and it wasn't true and he took her in his arms and held her very tightly to comfort her. She hadn't realised a big strong man could be so upset.

That night he told her they would have to leave Acrefield in the near future. They would live beside the sea and as soon as she could walk she would be able to paddle. He talked about her books and admired Eddie's violets and left her feeling happier, although a little perturbed because she loved Acrefield and Tom Tom and Eddie would be left behind. But to her the future was a long way off and there were many more days in which Eddie was to influence her own future far more than anyone else would.

Chapter 5

The war had ended. It was now 1920 and times were changing. There were more motor cars, and horses were no longer an integral part of almost every household.

When everyone was busy Elfie had to make her own world. In winter she enjoyed drawing in the nursery, the fire blazing, flames leaping to make intriguing shadows on the walls. If she looked deep into the flames she could see horses; horses jumping; horses flying; horses galloping; and horses speeding.

Speed.

They were free to race as she could never race; she tried to imagine being free to run. She drew horses running with the wind in their manes and tails, horses stretching their beautiful bodies, ecstatic with the thrill of movement.

Movement.

She dreamed of it more and more. She often spoke to Eddie of her imaginary pony galloping along the sands with her on its back. Or on the moors. Both were places she had never experienced except from a distance, marooned in her chair.

It was part of Eddie's job to help care for the ponies. He preferred working in the stables to helping in the garden; he enjoyed caring for the household animals; he loved the dogs. He watched the gleam in Elfie's eyes, the excitement and animation in her face as she told him of the wonderful moment when Ned had put her on Nancy and she had been riding. Really riding.

Poor little moppet. She might be the young lady of the house but she felt as he did about horses; and she hadn't much of a life. He had an idea. It mightn't work, but he'd try it. He might get into terrible trouble; he might be sacked; but if it did work it would be worth it. He found his opportunity one bright summer day. Would he wheel Miss Elfie out? Everyone else was very busy and she ought to have a change of scene.

He wheeled her round to the stables. Nobody was about. She was delighted when she discovered their destination. She could talk to the pony. Eddie parked the wheelchair.

'Now, you just sit still and wait a bit, Miss Elsie,' he said.

'What are you going to do?'

He grinned at her. He was nearly as excited as she would soon be.

'Ask me no questions and I'll tell you no lies,' he said. It was a frequent saying. Everyone said it to her at some time or another.

She watched Eddie, quite mystified. He brought the pony into the yard, which was normal enough. He found a blanket, folded it thickly and put it on the pony's back. He had put the bridle on; and attached a leading rein. A strap round its neck; and then he came out with a surcingle.

He lifted Elfie from her chair.

'Upsadaisy,' he said, and she found herself, totally astonished, sitting on Frosty's back, with the surcingle fastened over her knees and round the pony to hold her tight. Eddie took the leading rein.

'Hang on,' he said, and, very gently, began to walk the pony.

She was riding. The leg irons were almost forgotten; she had thought the pony might not like them but he didn't seem to notice. It was a strange sensation, there on his back, his body moving under hers, bumping her gently. Each part of him seemed to move in a different direction.

She had only sat on Nancy while she was standing still. All the rest was her imagination. The big Shire mare had been in the stable.

She could stroke his mane; she could see more than she had ever seen around the stable yard; she was taller than Eddie; she was in heaven. Any moment now a fairy godmother would arrive and wave her wand and she would be transformed into a normal little girl with legs like anyone else's and off she would go, hunting across the fields, leaping high over every obstacle, the best rider of them all.

People would admire her. Admire her daring; admire her mastery of the horse; and admire her ability to control even the most fiery stallion. Her name would be on every lip.

Eddie said little, aware of some at least of her feelings. Watching her, he knew that even if he were discovered and sacked without a reference, which was the worst thing that could happen to anybody in his position, this moment would have been worth it, all of it.

It was time to go in.

Elfie screamed. She wanted to stay there, to go on riding, not to return to the hated basketchair.

'Hush,' Eddie said, desperate not to be found out. 'If anyone hears you and finds out what I did I'll get into terrible trouble; they might sack me. And you will never be able to ride Frosty again.'

There was instant silence. Nobody must ever know; not even Tom Tom. It was their secret and she could only ride Frosty when nobody else was around. They would have to be very careful.

Elfie would rather have her tongue cut out in best pirate tradition than lose the chance to ride.

She went into tea, blissfully happy, reliving every moment of her brief adventure and longing for the next time.

It was the first secret that she had kept from her father.

Chapter 6

The rides on Frosty the trap pony continued. They became more and more exciting, as Elfie soon discovered she could ride the pony by herself and she begged to be let off the leading rein. She was a big girl, not a baby.

She could control Frosty. She could guide him in any direction she chose. She could go where she liked, and one day, adventuring too far, their secret was discovered.

Eddie was white-faced and stammering, Elfie prepared to be stopped for ever from riding her beloved pony. But to her astonishment her parents and Nanny were delighted. They watched her, realising the sheer pleasure this was giving her and also that it was possibly an escape from the chair, a venture into a more normal life. Her father was so overjoyed that he went straight out and came home with a riding bridle and a whip for her.

Eddie was promoted to taking Elfie out on the pony. Riding became a daily event, at eleven every morning, and she couldn't wait for the slow hours to pass. They ventured out of the grounds and into the fields; fields that up to then it had been impossible for her to visit as the ground was too rough for the chair. There was so much to see.

Trees and bushes and reeds by the river; flowing water and growing buttercups and cowslips, riotous in the grass. She could see over the hedges to poppies in the corn. The whole world lay in front of her, waiting to be explored. She had never been so happy in her life. While on the pony she almost forgot pain. The family watched her begin to come out of her shell, to show a wild desire to be out on Frosty, chattering excitedly about all she had seen on her rides and about her pony. Her riding whip always went up to bed with her, lying on the chair where she could see it.

Life was still painful but at last it was worth living. There was something to look forward to. Frosty was naughty and not always well-behaved but she adored him: he was more important to her than almost anything else in her world. Eddie became increasingly more proud of her progress as she learned to jog and sometimes rode off by herself among the trees in the grounds, almost out of sight of adults for the first time in all her life.

It was freedom; it was a chance to be alone, to be herself, to find out what kind of person she was. Not Elfie always in the way, always having to be shifted from one place to the other, always being carried by adults as if she were still a baby, but now she could plan to cross the lawn and actually cross it without having to wait for someone to push her or carry her. She could select a gravel path, leading to the end of the garden and go down it. She did not have to ask anyone; only tell Frosty where he was to go and he obeyed her, giving her the legs she lacked, the chance to get up and go that she had not known for the past four years. She had completely forgotten what it felt like to run around.

She had no fear whatever of the pony. She rode out with Eddie beside her, and one summer day, as they came out of the gate, she realised there were a number of people about, all staring at her. Elation seized her. Here she was, the poor little crippled girl that everyone pitied and she was riding and they could only watch. They couldn't ride!

She held her head high and rode proudly, convinced they were admiring her wonderful prowess. She was galloping at night in her mind, reliving a daring adventure, achieving a sense of personality she had lost. They needn't pity her any more. She could do something that Nanny couldn't do, and Ellen couldn't do, and nor could Cook or the butler. She could ride, like her parents and be as good as they were any day.

Frosty was often bored by their jogtrots and when he was bored, he rolled. It didn't hurt Elfie because her leg irons protected her. And when he rolled, she used the whip that

41

she had never had the opportunity to use at any other time, punishing him for his sin.

He got up at once and trotted off and Eddie, always on foot, had to race to catch up. Elfie, with a chance to show off and be naughty, delighted in the performance which became more frequent and was often put in by the bus stop, where there was always a small crowd waiting.

Eddie never realised that both his charge and her pony had a sense of audience, a desire to play to the crowd, and that, for Elfie, to be able to impress people in this way was sheer bliss. He scolded her, but the rolling and the whipping and the trot afterwards as the pony got up, went on.

Eddie used to grin and one day he told her what was being said: 'That little crippled girl. Managing that wild pony that rolls and tries to get rid of her!'

Elfie was delighted when he told her, but added that the crowd would soon realise the pony was rolling on her leg irons and she couldn't even feel him.

Success was going to Elfie's head.

'Take the leg irons off,' she commanded.

It proved a battle as she had never put them on or taken them off. The buckles were stiff and unmanageable, the straps seemed to go into the oddest places and were more like a jigsaw puzzle, and the whole lot slotted down into the brown surgical boots.

They fought the wretched things, laughing and furious at the same time. They were so impossibly unmanageable. At last they came off but they had no idea where to hide them, so Eddie rolled them up inside his jacket.

'Yer boots 'as got 'oles in,' Eddie said, and Elfie got those off and added them to the other hidden trophies.

She was as light as thistledown, sitting there on the pony, riding for the first time in her life without the hated leg irons. She began to show off and Eddie watched her, showing off with her, as they rode to the gate and people came to look at her, all admiring her, riding there as easy as kiss your hand and no leg irons. She didn't even feel a cripple any more. She sat easily, holding the reins, flourishing her whip, feeling like a queen.

Eddie felt as proud as if he was riding himself.

'Told you them legs would work, didn't I, Miss Elsie?' he said.

She looked back at the people they passed. There was no pity, no charity, just sheer admiration for her courage and the way she coped with a far-from-easy pony.

They rode further than usual and then it was time to go home. In the drive, the elation vanished and a feeling of misery returned.

'Eddie,' she said, 'did we cheat? Am I just pretending again?'

'We didn't cheat, honest,' he said. 'But there's no way we can get them things back on your legs and I don't know what they'll say.'

They both visualized a severe scolding with Eddie's ever-present bogy of the sack without a reference.

Eddie went in first and without a word unrolled his jacket and spilled the callipers and boots on to the floor. Everyone stared at them and he went out and brought Elfie in, carrying her and settling her in the big armchair in the hall, while those present stared even harder.

Eddie explained. He waited for anger, but his tale was received with delight. Elfie need only wear the callipers when practising walking.

'But what made you do it?' her father asked.

'Frosty keeps rolling while she's on him,' Eddie said, always truthful and unable to hide the real facts.

'Well,' Tom Pollok said, looking at his anxious small daughter. 'You two are having so much fun and Elfie looks so much better I think we will have to find another pony, one that behaves a bit better.'

A new pony. A pony of her own and not the trap pony that she had to share.

She was so excited she could barely sleep.

At last her own pony came: Patsy, an omen of the future many years ahead as yet, although Elfie had no idea of that.

Patsy was an enchanting little Welsh Mountain pony with pretty manners and a pretty head.

Best of all, when she came Eddie was bought a new outfit, and very smart he looked when he was out with her in his boots and gaiters, jacket and cap. Not much more than a child himself, he could share in her exultation and strut beside her, aware of his own importance while she, off her pony a shy mouse and sometimes sure everyone thought she was mental, on her pony was a different person, full of confidence and happiness, laughing and exultant, and just as good as everybody else.

She thought the good days would never end. She had never been so happy. She was content enough to accept her indoor existence if only she had her ride. She had forgotten her father had said they might have to move.

She knew nothing of failing economies, of the slump and the unemployed and the gathering gloom over the family as the rope business began to go downhill; money became tight; economies had to be made; and at last Acrefield had to be sold and they moved away.

There was no more Eddie.

She was desolate.

Chapter 7

Acrefield was a large residence and needed a huge staff to maintain it. There was the outdoor staff as well, the grooms in the stables, the kennel lads, and there was a style of living and entertaining that went with the house. The war was over, the slump had begun and everywhere the landed gentry were finding times very hard indeed.

It was difficult to accept the change as the new house was hideous. It was a Victorian seaside monstrosity, three-storeyed, badly proportioned, with a turret on one corner.

The inside was as ugly as the outside, and to a child who had grown up in spacious surroundings and beautifully proportioned rooms, the lack of space and of elegance jarred on her very artistic sensibilities.

The children were sent to stay at the rectory during the move and did not follow the family to the new home until it was fully furnished and decorated. It was only when they were installed that Elfie realised she had not been allowed to say goodbye to Tom Tom and Eddie.

Everyone hated the place. Worst of all to children used to spacious grounds, the only garden was a scrubby wilderness scoured by the salty winter winds, where most plants died and only the most hardy flourished. The garden ended in a seawall and beyond were the beach and the sea.

Elfie, as she spent so much time bed-bound, was given the turret room which had an allround view. She could look out at the ever-changing sea, at the little fishing boats setting out and returning, and at the flying gulls.

Her mother had given a great deal of thought to its decoration, so that she had an enchanting wallpaper and exotic chintz curtains covered in birds and flowers. But it was a lonely room, isolated from the rest of the house and from other people, and for the rest of her life the memory of that turret room emphasized the difference between her and the other children.

There were no stables. Patsy, her new pony, and the trap were kept a mile away with a man to look after the pony. A gardener came once a week but it was hardly worth his while as the wind blew sand over the grass, which was rough and scrubby; the wind also stunted the trees and killed the flowers.

There was always wind. It whined round her windows at night and when she woke in the dark hours it reminded her of an injured animal, crying its misery, tormented, as she was, by life.

The other children were at school, the boys at boarding school, and she was lonelier than ever. Her father was beginning to drink heavily now and could not always come to her. He was sometimes beyond conversation. But when he wanted company he found it in his small daughter. He was able to communicate with her as he could with no one else; she needed him so desperately and helped him a great deal by her need.

She could see the grass behind the house from her window. Sometimes it was a cricket pitch and sometimes a tennis court, and the kennels were at the far end.

There were always dogs; the bitches had pups that went to the Scottish estates to be trained for the gun and then came home. Dogs that would sit by her and lean their heads against her, giving her brief company until they felt the need to get up and move about, something denied to her.

Sometimes her father would forget she was a child and talk to her of things that were difficult to understand. Of things that perhaps worried him desperately as Elfie came to be more and more important to him.

'Your mother and I are cousins,' he said one day.

'Is that different?' the child asked.

'Doctors say cousins shouldn't marry as they might have handicapped children.'

'Am I handicapped?'

46

He was appalled by his tactlessness.

'No. You are not. Stupid people might think you are but you must never take offence. They are ignorant and tactless, but you must understand and forgive them. They are to be pitied, *not* you. You'll be hurt, often, but remember, you are what you want to be. Always. You can dream, you can make up stories, draw pictures, escape to a world busier people will never be lucky enough to know; you have time; time to fantasize; you are very special to me now, and when you are grown up you will be special to other people too. You may be can't walk; what does it matter? You can read more, learn more, talk more, listen more than other children; you can watch the moon ride up the sky and the stars come out, and think of all those strange worlds and perhaps of people on them; you can see the wind run through the trees; you can learn to have faith in yourself; keep that faith, in *you*. You've patience and understanding now beyond your years; never give up. Be like the Browning poem: to thine own self be true. And always, help others.'

'How can I help others? I can't walk.'

'That's why you can help. You're my help now; my special one, that keeps me sane. You know I'm drunk sometimes, and you probably know I'll get drunker before long; but you don't care, you're my friend and very precious to me.'

They weren't always in agreement; they were too alike, both passionate and could fight with words for days. But always he was ready to explain books that baffled older children, the books he chose for her to stretch her mind as her body could never be stretched, books of Greek mythology, of adventure, of travel; books on history and autobiographies, books on birds and wild life, on geography and architecture, on antiques and dogs and fishing, and on horses.

Horses.

His passion for horses was as great as hers. He could not explain it to her; he did not need to as she sensed it, and she knew he approved of her own obsession and gave her the chance to indulge it whenever she could.

47

He took her down to the farm to see the new calves and the lambs, the foals and the dogs, the chickens and the guinea fowl. He knew a great deal about farming and talked seriously to the men, who asked for his opinion on various matters, and discussed the market prices of store cattle and milking cows and the latest problems in the herd.

He took her down to the beach to see the fishing folk and visit their cottages on the shore. He carried her to the nets where the old men were busy, mending with gnarled fingers, exchanging tales of the sea. She grew to love the smell of the little boats; it was exciting to lie in the bottom of the 'Gladys' on her rug, amongst the tackle and the buckets and the damp.

The fishermen's wives gave them tea; brought out the best china and made scones and cakes and added plates of thin bread and butter and homemade jam. The man and the girl were equally at home in the poorer cottages, drinking happily out of enamel mugs, where the talk went on of the sea and fish. Sometimes they took her out in a rowing boat, where nobody else could move about much either. She was, more than most children, aware of the restless tumble and toss and heave and swell of the sea, of the white-topped waves and the excitement of being in a wider world than at home.

And then home, to recriminations from Nanny because the child's clothes were damp. She would catch her death; he never considered other people and all that washing made extra work. Her clothes were ruined. And she smelled of fish. It offended their sensitive noses. Such people as fishermen weren't fit for her to know.

She hated the rows, but such escapades were more than worth the unpleasantness that always followed them. Her father forced her to make efforts she might never have made without him, to give her hope and courage and the sheer grit to succeed. He tried to make her less sensitive, yet to use that sensitivity; and to make her use her brains and think as women of her class at that time rarely did.

'Life's never easy, love,' he said, often and often. 'Why should it be?'

And when she complained of pain or misery or loneliness or boredom, he held her tightly in his arms and told her that it was God's way of helping her to grow and be an even more special and understanding person.

'If you can live with it and not get bitter, you will be nicer than anybody I know,' he said.

She treasured his words as she treasured his visits. No one else ever bothered to spend so much time just talking with her; the rest of the family seemed to regard her as a chore or a duty. She was his treasure, his saving sanity, and the knowledge gave her the courage to fight against the infliction that God had so mysteriously sent to her.

If she asked her mother or the aunts and uncles they merely said that God moved in mysterious ways.

But her father answered: 'He chose you because you are special.'

She was determined that, come what might, she would walk, as he wanted. She would walk and she would ride. She would show them all.

She recited it at night in the windy room, with the sound of the waves crashing on the beaches and the howl of the gale, and the knowledge of men out there fighting the sea, as she was going to fight her useless legs. It became her litany.

Please God, help me to walk. Please God, help me to walk.

Chapter 8

Elfie's father gave her courage. He also gave her understanding. But it was to be many years before she even understood what her mother, her Nanny and Ellen had given her as she fought to walk.

They gave her anger.

Her mother came daily to her room with olive oil which she rubbed painfully into every inch of Elfie's useless legs. Rub, rub, rub, with a ferocity the child thought hard.

She took each leg and bent it, stretched it, bent it, straightened it, while the muscles responded with agonising pain that made the child cry. Crying was useless. The exercise went on. Sometimes Nanny took over, sometimes Ellen.

'You aren't trying, Elfie. Come on now. Try and do it by yourself.'

One of the outdoor staff took the seat out of a chair to make a standing frame, and she was put in it, to stand and try to move her legs by herself. The floor was of cork and the olive oil rubbed into her feet marked it; the floor for years was stained with the visible signs of the agonising daily efforts.

She was sure they didn't know how much it hurt, but she wanted to walk and when the pain was worst she would think of riding. Riding as no member of the family had ever ridden before; she would be a jockey and ride in races; she was a Sheikh in the desert riding his favourite mare. She was going to walk.

Standing and exercising and then one step. One step—it was all she could manage for weeks, and it hurt every time she did it. The first step is always the hardest, her father said, and laughed at her.

'Come on, lovey, you can do it,' Ellen said, supervising the daily agony.

'You're not trying,' Nanny said, over and over, in exasperation, determined that those legs would work, driving the child daily to make more effort, never mind if it did hurt.

She read Hans Andersen's *Little Mermaid* about the mermaid who gave up her tail in exchange for human legs, and all for love and walked for ever on knives that pierced her with every step. How well Elfie knew how she felt.

Walk, with the tears streaming down her face. It hurt.

Walk. They forced her once they knew she could take two steps; they fought her, they bullied her, they made her so angry she walked to spite them, to show them, to prove they were wrong when they said she wasn't trying, that she would never walk.

They goaded her and she hated them, unfeeling, unsympathetic, never praising the two steps, the three steps, but asking for more, more, more.

It wasn't until years later that she realised that her mother must have gone away to her own room and cried in lonely isolation, because she had to cause such pain. To the child they were all hard and bullying and she did not understand that they did it for her own good.

'I hate you,' she shouted at Nanny one day, and Nanny, looking down at her small charge, shrugged her broad shoulders and sighed.

'There's times you have to be cruel to be kind,' she said.

Elfie thought it the silliest expression she had ever heard.

To compensate there were riding lessons, but for some reason her mother's utter lack of any kind of understanding about clothes where this daughter was concerned made even those a misery in one way.

She was pushed round to the stables wearing thick serge bloomers, which were very rough and remarkably painful to a new rider; with brown leather gaiters that came over her knees, leaving a big gap as the bloomers slid up and the gaiters wrinkled downwards.

Her teacher was Jim Sudden, a tiny gnomish man who was always immaculately dressed so making her feel even more frumpish. She was now eleven years old.

She was lifted on to the horse. There was feeling in her legs, although they were useless for riding; she could sense the stirrup flaps and the buckle underneath which was painful, and exceptionally so in cold weather.

She wore a long covert coat and a velour hat, always tan gloves, and carried her beloved whip, the first riding gift her father had given her. It was a small stable, with only three big horses and two ponies, and Elfie was always given Judy, a bad-tempered little 13-hand mare.

Jim Sudden had to work out different ways to teach her. No heels down and stretch your legs and balance with your seat; at first, worried lest she fall, he put a padded rod across her legs, held down so that she was strapped on. But somehow she learned to balance, and then to use her hands on the neckstrap to rise into a trot. In no time at all they were riding for long treks across the beach and over the dunes; no need to dream, this was happening.

Sometimes, if Judy was unfit, she was heaved on to one of the big horses. She had no fear and the leg strap was soon discontinued. Jim Sudden coached her endlessly so that she improved all the time, and although no one realised it, the riding was bringing the useless muscles back into play and the walking across the nursery floor was becoming a little easier—but no less painful. Riding did not seem to hurt so much, or perhaps she enjoyed it so immensely that she could ignore the pain.

Jim Sudden was dedicated to trotting as a means of mastering the horse. Also, trotting made this pupil work to overcome her own rather daunting difficulties. From the first lesson it was: use your hands, carry your whip properly, use your hands, hands, use those hands. Handle both reins correctly. Small hands were no excuse. She had no aids through her legs, which the normal rider uses to guide the horse by exerting pressure, squeezing to a stop or nudging him right or left with the lower leg and heel, so that her whip had to substitute, pressing behind the stirrup, on the right side or the left, to guide the horse. She began to develop powerful arm muscles as all her riding had to be done with her arms. They trotted in this way for miles and she learned that she could think with the horse; although she had a great deal to learn, she had an understanding of the animal that had been born in her and that may never be learned by others, no matter how well they ride.

Unlike Eddie's daily rides, this was a once-a-week treat; an expensive treat, as lessons cost money and the household was economising in many ways. But no matter what other economies were made, the lessons went on. In between whiles she did ride Patsy occasionally, when someone had time to take her to the stable.

It meant a mile walk, with her father pushing the chair both ways, and then more time spent on the ride. It was a very tame ride after the adventurous sorties in the fields with Eddie. She missed Eddie and she missed Tom Tom, other people didn't seem able to share in her need for talk.

Slowly, she began to walk a little more: only a few steps, but it was a beginning and now the three women who were concerned to make her try were able to ease up a little and praise her on occasion for trying. She had new places to visit and different walks, and new sights and scenes, so that with fresh horizons and the weekly adventure with Jim Sudden her life began to hold more interest. Also as she grew older, she could use her active brain in different ways and learn to gain compensation from other skills.

Her greatest pleasure was reading; and on winter days, with a fire in the nursery and the wind howling round the house and the rain lashing down, it was cosy and comforting to be indoors and not forced outside as others were.

At first, she loved the sea: the summer sea with tiny waves lapping against the shore. And then she heard the women talk; and heard the siren yell as the lifeboat was summoned and stared from the window into the hellish torment of giant waves that thundered on the beach and she knew that out there, beyond sight of land, men were fighting for their lives, and sometimes lost the fight. Once or twice they were men she had known and spoken with, had had tea in their cottages. They would never walk the beach again or lift their small children high against the sky and laugh.

Reading, others had words to describe her feelings:

> *Full fathom five thy father lies,*
> *Of his bones are coral made.*

Sometimes the storms were beyond all reason, wild and terrifying, the sea thunderous, the wind rattling windows and doors and roaring like some untamed beast, challenging puny men to defy its strength. On such nights there were fishing boats driven on to the beach, or carried close to danger and to other wrecks. The beach was only a hundred yards away and when that happened all the household went out with blankets and brandy, with hot soup in flasks and first-aid equipment.

Elfie lay awake, alone in the big empty house, desperately wishing she could be down there, helping. That was something she never achieved except in day dreams. When at last all was well and the household about to settle to rest, her father, knowing she was awake, would come and tell her what had happened, and ease her fears, as by then the roar of the wind and the crash of the waves had achieved nightmare proportions, and she imagined the sea taking all the family from her and leaving her alone, unable to walk, to starve as no one remembered the helpless cripple in the turret room. She felt like a heroine or perhaps a victim from the novels of the Brontës: the hidden unwanted member of the family, tucked away in the attic, unacknowledged because they were ashamed of her.

Once she knew the family were all home and all safe in their beds, she could sleep even though the storm raged on and the wind wailed like a banshee around her turret windows.

She also began to paint, much more seriously. Little water-colours of sea and sand and sky; pictures of ships; and, of course, drawings of horses. They were much admired, as was Elfie's talent. She had a skill beyond her years and was very good indeed.

Encouragement helped, and she started detailed drawings of everything around her. They brought her flowers to paint and twigs, pussy willow and catkins of all kinds, and she began to enjoy her days. Her mind was occupied by the books her father brought her to read; and her increasing skill with her hands and the sketches that began to surround her helped overcome her shyness. She was also learning not to voice her thoughts to anyone but her father and Ellen, as what they didn't know they couldn't scold you for. And she did have some odd thoughts.

She hated the evenings and nights as sometimes they forgot her and she was left alone in the dark, unable to walk downstairs, unheard if she called and unable to read or draw. There was only the howl of the wind to listen to and the desolate sound of the waves against the shore, and fear of unnamed things that might hide in the corners of the room and pounce out at her. They did remember in time and came and switched the lights on for her, but no one ever realised how much she hated the dark.

Sometimes she was taken downstairs and her mother played to her, always playing Beethoven or Bach. Her mother was a good pianist but somehow the effect she produced on her daughter was of deep and dark depression and Elfie loathed the evening piano recitals and hated both composers for the rest of her life.

She was downstairs by day, but her mother seemed never to regard this daughter as anything but a very small child, possibly because she still had to be carried and could not walk more than a few steps across the nursery floor. So she was put to bed before the family dinner, an occasion for which everyone dressed in formal clothes, and had her own high tea before her bath. Bedtime was so early and she was not in the least tired.

The highlight of the day was 'Daddy after dinner'. He came up to her turret room, nearly always having primed himself with whisky first and bringing the port decanter with him. Both the visits and the port were a terrible sin. Time and again her mother and Nanny tried to intervene, but Elfie had discovered that she could sob herself into hysteria, putting on an act that terrified everyone into thinking she was far worse than she was, and behaving as if she were totally inconsolable and would become ill without his visits. It was true, but she did know how to create the kind of scene that got her her own way. So Mother and Nanny gave in and went away with compressed lips and her father stayed with her, amusedly aware of her naughtiness but not caring.

Sometimes he sang downstairs with her mother. But the songs he sang for Elfie when he came to keep her company in her lonely room were always Scottish ballads and songs of the old days, many of them wistful and romantic, feeding her imagination. Sometimes he sang in Gaelic, singing in a soft voice. Those were the evenings that she loved best of all.

She could never hear any of the songs in years to come without being taken back to the turret room and her father sitting beside her, brightening the lonely hours, able to take her with him into realms of imagination and wonder that no one else in her life ever knew, or could share with her.

By now too he was sharing her rides and when he could, he hired a horse and went with her, along the beaches and over the dunes, so that their long-ago dreams had become reality. 'You wanted to ride, and you have,' he told her, over and over, when she complained about her slow progress on two legs and the pain in her legs. 'Now you want to walk and you will walk. Remember, whatever you want to do, you can if you want it badly enough and try hard enough.'

She went on trying, enduring the pain, until she was walking across the room. She was walking further each day; she was fighting her rebellious legs. Often the pain was so bad she had to stop and lean against a wall, but she was going on.

She was going to walk.

And then she was going to work with horses and be the best rider ever.

Even her father smiled at that particular dream. But he kept his thoughts to himself, knowing that some dreams never do come true and this one did no harm as it would help her conquer her disability. And once she could walk and lead a more normal life the dream would be forgotten, as so many childhood dreams are forgotten.

Chapter 9

She was walking. Slowly, painfully, often creeping, often having to lean against a wall to blink away the tears that came into her eyes as her muscles rebelled against usage after being idle so long, but she was walking.

It was limited freedom as she limped, she lurched, and she felt as ungainly as a crab, but she was independent of other people. She could choose to sit by the fire, or walk across the room to sit by the window; she did not have to stay where she was put.

She could select a new book when the one she was reading was finished; she could fetch a fresh sheet of paper when she had completed a sketch; she could sit at table with the family. She had so much to learn about the ways of the household; the downstairs ways. She had never been part of those; only a visitor to them, lying on her settee, listening to talk that ignored her.

Now she was able to come and go to a limited extent as she pleased. And she could ride for miles with her father, when he felt able or was free from the demands of his work.

Elfie's wide reading had given her more understanding than she realised as she read about horses in the wild; the ever-hunted, running from danger, with a built-in instinct that was as old as time itself, teaching them to bolt from fear of the unknown that might threaten them. The horse, preyed-on by wolves in Europe long ago; the horse, racing from the wild beasts of the prairies and the pampas; Russian horses, running on the steppes, victims of wolf packs.

New Forest ponies, living free and gathered together and sold. What must it feel like to be brought in from the woods and the sky, into an auction ring, wild as any fox running in the woods, and be handled by men who had heavy hands and hard voices and only cared for money? Men who might whip or beat or kick? Men who did not stop to understand the beasts they handled.

Jim Sudden understood them. Her father understood them, and without knowing it she learned gentleness and patience. Patience was hard because she was often frustrated and unruly, but horses would not respond to bad temper; they would not obey and they might try to unseat a hated rider. She had to understand if she was going to be a first-class rider, and she was. She had to think like a horse and live with them, not just ride them. Her father helped her look after Patsy herself; and as soon as she was able to move around the house, he took her to the stable.

There, mucking out the dirty straw, putting down fresh bedding, fetching water, fetching hay, she learned the basics of stable management without knowing she was learning.

'Smell this hay, Elfie,' her father would say, 'It's musty. No good at all. Hay should smell sweet and fresh or it makes the horse ill.'

Her disability was still a challenge as the horses were used to being ridden by normal riders who could control their hindquarters by using their legs to give signals and guide the animal, and control their forequarters by their hands on the reins.

She delighted in learning. 'Make sure the horse is standing squarely and accepting the bit lightly,' 'Gently with your hands,' 'Obedience comes when the horse turns to the command of a leg,' but her command had always to be the tap of the whip, in exactly the right place, simulating the leg nudge. Her riding became more skilled and more satisfying.

Her father was her most constant companion. Nanny and Ellen were there to talk to, but her mother was a distant person now that the olive oil routine had ended.

Only once did Elfie ever hear her father make any comment on other people's manners. He had held a shooting party and invited some of the men to dinner, as he often did. Elfie was used to her parents entertaining but this was an extra grand occasion. Much too grand for Elfie to be present.

She watched the preparations: the house decked with flowers, the silver polished, the glassware gleaming, the damask cloth and the beautifully arranged table; the perfectly cooked meal that the cook and the household staff laboured to produce; the decorated sweets, all beautifully set out, topped with whipped cream, the carefully chosen wines.

She had her own meal alone, a bit of this and a bit of that brought to her by Ellen, and felt like Cinderella denied the ball.

She sat by the nursery fire, drawing, and then, hearing voices downstairs became curious and tiptoed out on to the landing to see the visitors: the men in evening dress, the women in lovely gowns that she envied. They were so sleek and elegant and poised, so sophisticated and so beautiful and her mother was like a fairy queen and the loveliest of them all.

Mirror, mirror on the wall, who is the fairest of them all? The answer had to be Elfie's mother.

She watched the peacock parade leave the dining-room and adjourn to the drawing-room, heard the bright voices and laughter, and no one was aware of the girl hiding on the landing. As they passed they were like fairy-tale creatures, with their jewels sparkling and the rich colours and materials; the beautifully dressed hair and the discreetly powdered faces.

They went into the drawing-room, which was decorated with carefully arranged flowers. Everything was spotless, as the indoor staff had slaved all day. Elfie wondered what they talked about, there behind the closed door. And what the men talked about as they passed the port and smoked cigars that left their smell behind long after the party was over.

Ellen and Nanny were both busy and she was bored. She stayed on the landing.

The phone rang.

Her father was called out to answer it, and, not bothering to lower his voice, continued with what he must have been saying a moment before: 'Damned tradesman. Damned tradesman.'

Elfie was fascinated but waited until the phone call was over before she spoke. She called down through the bannisters as he turned to go back into the dining-room and join the men again.

'Who's a damned tradesman, Daddy?'

He looked up at her.

'You shouldn't be there.'

'Well, I am. Who were you talking about?'

'His bloody Lordship, damn his eyes.'

'Why?'

'Because he thinks his stinking money can buy our land, our pheasants, our shooting ...'

He looked up at her, suddenly realising he was talking to a child.

'Can you get yourself back to bed?'

She was undressed but hadn't been in bed.

He looked up at her face, and raced up the stairs and carried her back to bed.

He tucked her up, bent to kiss her and then laughed.

'See?' he said. 'Strictly sober, and swearing. You never got out of bed so you didn't hear a thing, did you?'

'No, Daddy.' She smiled at him, the elfin smile that always enchanted him and he was aware of her huge eyes watching him as he went out of the room. It wasn't the first secret they had had and it wouldn't be the last. She heard him going down the stairs, still muttering 'Damned tradesman'.

By the time she was fourteen she was able to walk considerable distances, although still painfully and sometimes with a tremendous limp; on other days her legs seemed to behave and she started ballet lessons. They were painful too and she became more than ever aware of ungainliness. That odd girl with the peculiar walk. But at least that was better than being poor Elfie, in the bath chair with the cloche hat and the veil. She still remembered that, although her clothes were now very pretty.

She had never been to school, but her father had ensured

that she was far more widely read than any other girl of her age; she had had a much more liberal education, without even knowing she had been educated.

The family had decided that her elder sister could have her wish and become a nurse. Her brothers would go into the rope-making factory. But what could poor Elfie do?

'Look after horses,' said Elfie.

'Don't be stupid. As if you could do that sort of thing!'

Some days later, as Elfie went out of the room, leaving the door open behind her, Ellen said,'Born in a barn, Miss Elfie?' It was an everyday saying, and she shut the door and suddenly thought how lovely it would have been to be one of the children in the village and born in a barn and not have to mind her manners and be seemly. And then she could work with horses.

For some reason Elfie never understood, any new departure for any member of the family was the subject for family discussion. Elderly uncles and aunts seemed to descend in droves and give their opinions on the future of the children.

Elfie should not spend so much time riding; she had a talent. They collected her sketchbooks and discussed her drawings. A young lady might well be permitted to earn a little pin-money by illustrating children's books, perhaps, and doing a few little delicate and pretty watercolours. Elfie should go to Art School in Liverpool.

She went to Art School.

Chapter 10

Art School had one benefit — although she could not see it at the time. It made her use her legs. Walk to the station, take a train, often standing as it was full, walk through Liverpool to the School. It took ages, at a very slow pace, still having to think about making her legs move, driving them to obey her will, unable ever to forget them. Often she felt she couldn't complete the journey as her muscles ached so much and she had to stop several times and lean against a fence or post or wall to ease the agony. Nobody realised how much her legs hurt, but since she would never lead a normal life if she didn't walk, she walked.

She hated the School. Her mother, having somehow missed out on Elfie's schoolgirl days, seemed not to realise that this was an adult school, not for children, as the school-leaving age at the time was fourteen and Elfie was fourteen. She was sent to her classes embarrassingly and absurdly dressed in a dark coat and velour hat and a gym tunic and blouse.

No one else wore uniform and silly Elspeth in her baby clothes was a constant butt for the malicious and spiteful, who enjoyed teasing her and mimicking her and made her life total hell. She did make one very good friend who tried to protect her, and who remained a friend for all of her life. The only consolation was that she could draw; she did have a talent and the teachers helped her to develop it.

She was at ease in the stables as nowhere else. Patsy was her comforter; the pony had to be fed and cleaned up and groomed; standing there with the dandy brush in her hand and the soft coat against her cheek, and the warm breath on her face as the mare turned to watch her, looking into the dark deeply fringed wise eyes, Elfie was at peace as she never was at home, or at the School.

It was a deep satisfaction, but she could never explain it to anyone. They would not understand.

Her home life was becoming even more difficult, too, as her mother became very ill and was bed-ridden. Nobody seemed to know what was wrong with her. One of the aunts descended on them to manage the household; Elspeth had to behave with even more propriety than with her mother, or she earned herself a sarcastic lecture that reduced her to silent tears. She took refuge more and more often in her room, with her books and her sketchbook. As far as the aunt was concerned she was still a child, and an awkward and tactless child. She knew too that her father was earning more and more disapproval as he, reduced to as much misery as his daughter by the iron rule of the disciplinarian aunt, spent his time alone in his snug, the bottle at his side.

When they could, they rode, but Elfie's riding companion these days was George, who took out visiting riders. She didn't know George well but he accepted her as she was, helped her to improve her riding, and she regarded him as one of her very few friends, as he was never critical or sarcastic.

She never did get used to loudly spoken, unkind comments from passers-by or other girls who meant her to overhear what they said. She became wary and suspicious and often felt like a horse herself, having to face up to life, but wanting to bolt. She tried not to mind, but she never grew out of her sensitivity. She learned to present a brave face to an uncaring and often malicious world.

She didn't want pity; she just wanted to be accepted as a normal person and not as being different; that funny little cripple.

She daydreamed about riding, but now, in her daydreams, she was not Elfie; she was the boy she should have been, free to go about as men did, no longer chaperoned and made to remember she had to be careful because she was a girl and terrible things could happen to girls who went about

64

alone or who were free and easy with men. Nobody ever said exactly what would happen. She could not ask her mother who suffered from extreme weakness and a lack of interest in the world around her. To have her busy energetic mother confined to her bed all the time was extremely upsetting and rather frightening, as she might die; and then there would only be the aunt for ever.

Elfie was used to the dogs dying, in one way, but not to the finality of their absence and it would be so much worse if her mother died. The thought plagued her at night, lying in bed, wishing she could leave college and work with horses, and not be dressed in her stupid ugly clothes.

She could escape so briefly now to ride.

She drew. For homework she had to draw a variety of things that did not interest her, although she did enjoy doing one example of a Chinese ornament, a fan-shaped picture of a very Chinese-looking horse flying above stylised clouds with a decorated margin, the horse distinctly unhorselike yet alive with movement.

Another was a design for a Persian carpet, with antlered stags feeding, one leaping, one standing, wary, head raised and turned over his shoulder, watching for danger, against a background of growing unlikely-looking formal plants and very Victorian bowls of flowers.

For her own pleasure she drew horses; skeletons of horses, to show the bones; drawings of the hindleg and the foreleg with each bone named; the muscles of the horse, in loving, extremely careful detail, good enough for any book illustration on anatomy.

She did a wish-fulfilment sketch of Jim Sudden on a day when she couldn't ride, a neat man with a big nose and a trim moustache and a bowler. She wished she could ride every day.

Nanny still lived with them and she and Ellen tended to treat Elfie as a little girl at times; her aunt always treated her as if she were about ten. The other people in college were much older than she and so were more mature, more sophisticated and often alarming.

65

She could not get excited about designing Persian carpets; she drew accurate and elegant pen drawings of leaves and twigs, of catkins and flowers; some were used to illustrate a book on plants, and she was paid a pittance for her illustrations, but it meant nothing whatever. It did not even thrill her although everyone else was delighted — Elfie might make it at last.

She was only alive when she was riding. She was gaining skill all the time, was learning without realising it because she picked George's brains and Jim Sudden's brains, absorbing their experiences, envying them their expertise and their strong legs, although she was now able to use her legs instead of her whip most of the time.

Also, although she did not realise it, she was walking faster and more normally, and her legs did not ache quite so much. But pain was still a daily reminder of her years spent lying on a bed or a couch, or being wheeled in a chair.

Her drawing improved, and always her pictures of animals came to life while those of plants remained stilted, although very good of their kind, especially for a fifteen-year-old. A polar bear on an ice floe, standing poised, ready to dive into the water. A monkey's head, the monkey with a quizzical look in his eyes, summing up humans and finding them amusing. A delightful brush drawing of a scruffy little mongrel, sitting with his back to her, entranced by something happening in front of him, every muscle tense, about to leap up and investigate, his ears cocked in interest. A ten-minute sketch of a sultry sky, and boats at anchor on the water, a hint of a rocky shore, a soft blur of colours.

It was no good. She was only alive when she was riding. Nobody understood.

She loved poetry and remembered Milton:

And that one talent which is death to hide,
Lodged with me, useless.

She didn't want to remember the rest of it. It described so perfectly what she felt. She was born to ride. Why couldn't they understand? Why did she have to be a girl? Who wanted to be a girl? You couldn't go anywhere by yourself, you couldn't do anything, you wore idiotic clothes and were supposed to behave like a lady. Who the hell wanted to be a lady? She wanted to be a stable boy and to ride and go where she pleased, to know a freedom denied to women. It was a stupid senseless beastly world and she hated it.

But at least there was her once-a-week lesson and George. And then, one day, there wasn't even George. He had joined Blackpool Circus.

The circus!

She couldn't bear it any longer. If she took her pocket money and added it to her college money she could get to Blackpool, especially if she waited for the cheap-day train.

She arrived at the circus and George was horrified, sure he was the victim of an idiotic schoolgirl crush from this silly little creature. The Italian wife of the strong man took pity on her, and George, having told the circus people where her family lived, kept well away from her, afraid he would be thought to have enticed her. She wasn't the first child to be entranced by the circus and wouldn't be the last, but few of them ever ran away.

She watched the horses rehearsing; the bareback riders with their perfect balance, the sweep and swing of the ride as the animals went through their act. She saw them in the stables, beautiful white horses with flowing manes, groomed to perfection.

She would work with them, clean them, groom them, feed them, learn to ride as the slender girls rode them. The girls smiled at the tiny ungainly child, still dressed in her absurd tunic, with legs that did not work as they should, and were also much shorter than they would have been had she grown normally. But, under the Señora's stern eye, they were kind.

The Señora was motherly, and sorry for this odd waif, wondering what had induced her to run away from home. She heard about the sick mother and the Art School and the longing to ride, and did the only thing she could do — produced a mountainous meal. She could offer little consolation as her English was not good and she had not

67

understood much of the story; only recognised the misery.

She had watched the girl's face as she stood by the horses and known that here was a passion that would never be fulfilled, and was sad for her, but the parents must have their child back.

Her father came that evening. He did not scold. He said very little, and thanked the circus people for their kindness and for calling him. He also thanked George and reassured him, so that he knew he was not blamed for Elfie's escapade.

Later, on the platform, waiting for the train, he turned and looked down at her.

'Oh, Elfie, Elfie. What *are* we going to do with you?' His voice had never sounded so sad.

Next day she took her usual train to Art School.

The years stretched before her, miserable and unrewarding. The dreams faded, to be replaced by an apathy that kept her moving, kept her legs working, but that took away all enthusiasm because she could never do what she wanted with her own life.

Chapter 11

The world that she knew ended very suddenly one bleak
March day.

It was not her mother who died.

It was her father.

He had a major coronary.

His death shocked everyone. He was only fifty-two.

For Elfie, it was the end of her life too. There was no one
now who would understand her at all. No one to share her
pleasure in her books; no one to laugh with, as none of the
rest of the family seemed to have any sense of humour at all.
She had never realised that you could live in a house full of
people and be so utterly lonely that the loneliness was agony.

Her mother was still an invalid. He aunt showed sympathy, but Elfie's problems were beyond her understanding.
She would miss her father, of course; it would be terrible if
she didn't, but she had to understand that she must lead a far
more normal life. The family were now trustees, deciding
the future for all of them. There had to be major changes in
their lifestyle. Her sister was no problem, nor were her two
brothers, the older now working, the younger doing well at
school. But what would they do with Elfie, the odd one out,
the misfit?

Her pony had to be sold for a start.

The solicitors arranged for him to go to a sale in a month's
time. Her father had replaced Patsy with a larger pony, and
he would fetch some money at least. After that they would
see about some sort of training for Elspeth, and perhaps
without the stable to escape to, she would become a credit to
the family and not a liability.

Wandering round the house like a lost soul, she didn't
know if her night-time tears were for her dead father or the

loss of her pony, the only remaining link with the life that she had known. She felt as she had as a child: superfluous and constantly in the way as everyone was busy, everyone seemed to have some kind of purpose in life, and she had none. She was existing in a terrible kind of limbo. It was useless talking to aunts, or uncles, or solicitors, and her mother was too ill to endure more than brief visits and a quick kiss, which was rewarded with a languid smile and a little conversation. She was very weary.

Elfie, trying to come to terms with the loss of her father, quite suddenly grew up. She knew if she didn't do something she wanted to do, she would spend the rest of her life being organised into doing things she hated, and be right back at the beginning, a non-person, trying to fit into a mould that didn't suit her. Even though she could now walk fairly well, she would be under somebody, ordered to do or don't, told how to behave, how to dress, forced to be seemly and 'refined' (shades of Miss Pierce haunting her still), and there would be no pony to escape on.

And no father to talk to, and to help her to accept her constricted life.

She was so isolated that she did not know how to bear it.

She was not going to be the family problem. She was going to make her own life, as she wanted it and not as they wanted it. She didn't know how, she only knew that her mind was finally made up. There was no one now to restrain her or to caution her, or to tell her to wait and something would turn up. Nothing would turn up. The Lord helped those who helped themselves.

First of all, Rory her pony would not go to a sale. She would sell him personally. It would be like selling half of herself. It had to be done. He wasn't a loveable pony; he was an awkward beast, and although good and sensible in traffic and quiet in the stable, he was a devil to shoe.

He would be sensible for days and a joy to ride and then for no apparent reason would nap or rear, or try with the most tremendous buck to unseat his rider. He needed understanding, especially as he had a few interesting variations on

70

the buck. He might precede it with a fly jump, repeated until either the rider came off or he decided he had taught her a sufficient lesson for the time being and resumed his happy behaviour. He would trot on lazily, a slow jog trot, at his own speed, until his mood changed and he became a rodeo pony again. She had always ridden alone, or only with her father riding beside her on his bicycle on their way to her jumping field, and she did wonder if he might behave better in company.

She wanted to take him herself and make sure his buyer knew his ways. She could not think where to sell him, but one morning the gardener, who also had to leave, was asking for a reference as he was applying for a job. An ex-cavalry man had started a riding school nearby and wanted a man to 'make up' the paddock and also put up a few jumps and act as general handyman, tidying the grounds and the yard.

It sounded possible. His name was Sergeant Edward Jones, late of the Denbigh Hussars, at Birch Road, Oxton.

She told no one. This was her pony and her affair.

It was too far to walk so she rode Rory.

Mr Jones already had four ponies; three of them 14 hands, one 12 hands, and yes, he would like a bigger pony for himself. He watched Elfie show Rory off; he liked his manners, as he did behave for once, and he was intrigued by the fact that this strong well-muscled animal was so easy to handle as his rider was tiny and looked delicate. She was an elf of a girl.

Elfie explained Rory's funny ways and watched the Sergeant ride him in the paddock for an hour. She stood at the gate, praying her pony would do nothing wrong, as she thought this would be a kind place for him. But she didn't want to sell him without Mr Ted Jones knowing what to expect; that would be most unfair and probably unwise too.

'I'll take him. Fifteen pounds.'

She couldn't take so little. She summed up all her courage and asked for thirty-five pounds.

'Tell you what,' the sergeant said. 'Leave him on trial for

71

two days. I can see how he goes; you won't have the stable work, so it will give you a break. But I can't pay your price, haven't got it.'

Elfie looked at the stables: they were beautifully kept, everywhere was clean and trim and showed that work went into the place. The other ponies were fit, in shining health. She agreed.

There was no bus home. Ted Jones offered to ride with her while she rode Rory and then to bring him back, but she decided to leave her pony behind and set off walking, on the long trek home.

She told no one of her day's work. Next day she set off as usual, pretending to 'do' the pony that was no longer there. She looked at the empty stable. She couldn't bear it.

She walked to Birch Road, helped exercise the ponies and muck out the stables, and felt her misery lighten. She was happy for the first time since her father died. It was almost her sixteenth birthday.

Then, at the end of the morning the Sergeant saddled Rory and took him into the paddock. Rory was in one of his worst moods; he bucked, he kicked, he fly jumped; he cavorted like a rodeo horse; he did his best to get the man off and Elfie watched in dismay while his rider sat him waving his felt hat in the air, as if he were the hero at a rodeo show. There was no chance that she could sell him now.

'Oh, Rory, you great fool,' she thought. 'If only you'd try. That's that.'

She watched the sergeant dismount and come up to her, with Rory's reins in his hand.

'Well?' he asked.

Elfie had no answer. Well, what? Well, yes? Well, no? The man looked at her unhappy face.

'Well, are you going to sell him to me?'

'I thought you hadn't enough money.'

He laughed.

'I'll drop to thirty as he behaved so badly,' she said hopefully.

'Twenty-five. Take it or leave it.'

72

She couldn't take it; it wasn't enough. And then the idea hit her, and she looked up at him longingly.

'I'll drop the price if you take me as well as the horse.'

He stared at her in astonishment.

'What on earth would I do with you, and where would I put you?' he asked.

'I want to learn. I want to work with horses. I don't know much. I looked after Rory though, when he left the livery stable; we didn't have enough money to keep him there. My father's died and we can't keep Rory and we need money badly. I'll work hard, honest.'

He had seen her ride the awkward little horse. He had seen the neat professional way she had tackled the stables, for all her size and her very odd walk. On foot she was clumsy, on the horse she was an angel. If she could manage as awkward a ride as this beast she had potential. And he could do with more help.

'OK. You're on,' he said. 'I'll buy Rory and your hours are eight a.m. to five p.m. Lunchtime off and wages half a crown a week to start with.'

If she could have danced she would have done so, but instead she could only beam at him and start for home, lugging her saddle and bridle, trudging wearily over the ground. It was too far to carry the saddle and she turned back, and left it at the stables for use.

She stood looking at Tregona, the prettiest little blood pony she had ever seen. She needed a rest before starting off for home again.

'Want to ride her?' Ted Jones asked, watching his new stable girl's face.

'May I?'

She didn't need a second invitation. She rode the pony round the yard and then into the paddock and jumped her. It was heaven. After Rory's awkward unpredictable ways it was so easy and she didn't want to get off or go home. She stabled the pony and made her comfortable and then set to work to clean her tack.

There was an easy silence; a companionable huffing, a

73

rich smell reminding her of the days spent with her father and the Shire horses; a feeling of pressure lifted and of coming home. The tack gleamed with her rubbing, and she left the tack room neat and shipshape.

She was very late, but her feet seemed to speed over the ground and she was longing to tell everyone of her achievement. She had sold her pony; she had twenty-five pounds for him and she had a job.

She almost ran into the house to tell them.

There was an outraged silence. She was talking to a group of people with stony faces, staring at her as if she had committed the worst outrage in the world. They couldn't have been more appalled if she had announced she had committed murder.

'You had better go to your room, Elspeth. There is no point in continuing this conversation.'

She didn't go to her room. She went to find Madeline, who was Ellen's replacement.

Madeline didn't understand either.

Yes, the pony did have to be sold, and that was a good thing done. But young ladies from our family and our kind of home never work in stables. It's a terrible thing to do.

'They did during the war.'

'That was different. Now go and change for dinner and don't let us hear any more of this nonsense.'

She didn't want dinner. She didn't want to change. But that would make matters worse so she struggled into her best dress, and was halfway into it when there was a bang on the door. Her aunt stalked in.

'Elspeth, I have to talk to you.'

She was at an immediate disadvantage, half in and half out of the dress, and stood, unable to speak, listening to an endless tirade that grew shriller and shriller. She was letting the family down; she could always be relied on to try something impossible; she couldn't possibly understand what a terrible crime she was committing, to work in a stable like a common groom, no lady could ever do such work. It was time she gave up this nonsense with horses and settled down to behave like a normal person; her father had ruined her and heaven alone knew what her poor mother would say, if only her poor mother were well, then we'd see.

Elspeth, who, only fifteen, had honestly thought the family would be pleased with her enterprise, could only stand there paralysed with horror. She could not see what was so dreadful. It was only after the aunt had gone, slamming the door behind her, having completely lost her temper and failed to get a word out of her niece, that Elfie realised she was still half in and half out of the dress.

She pulled at it, almost tearing it in her haste, and stormed off in fury to her mother's room. She had had enough of the aunt and her tantrums and her sarcasm and her insistence on the family honour. It sounded like *Beau Geste* but being a girl she couldn't run away and join the Foreign Legion. She wished she could. Why was she born a girl? Why was she born into a family that couldn't do anything normal? She couldn't even live the way she wanted to.

Her mother was so ill that a hospital nurse looked after her, a starchy daunting ogress who terrified Elfie. But tonight she didn't care. The aunt's tirade had enraged her to such a pitch that she was impervious to anyone's feelings. She pushed past the outraged nurse and into her mother's room.

Her mother was lying breathless, a tiny frail memory of herself, leaning against piled-up lace pillows.

Elfie spilled out her story, but almost before she had begun the nurse was there, trying to pull her out of the room, dragging at her clothes, while the girl became semi-hysterical, needing her mother desperately and unable to get out any words at all as an infuriated whispering went on, almost an echo of her aunt.

'Get out of here at once. What do you think you're doing?'

By now the aunt had arrived and the room was as peaceful as the centre of a thunderstorm with words shrieking from one person to the other, and Elfie standing, refusing to move, although both women were now trying to push her out.

'Elspeth,' her aunt began, in the well-known dreaded voice of doom.

Her mother pushed herself up on the pillows.

'Be quiet, both of you, and let the child speak.'

Both women stared at her, but held their tongues.

Her mother, flushed and angry, looked at her daughter.

'Now sit down, and tell me quietly what all this is about.'

Miserably, Elfie repeated the saga.

'You'd have done the same,' she ended. 'You wouldn't have let Rory go to just anyone who bid for him at a sale.'

'Yes,' her mother said. 'I probably would. But there is one thing. Before you start work I would like someone to go along and see Sergeant Jones and see if he is a respectable person. Also someone else should be working there with you, you can't possibly work alone with a man.'

Elfie stared at her mother and then grabbed her, hugging her until she protested, laughing, that she could scarcely breathe. Her mother smiled up at her. She was exhausted by the noise and the scene, but she managed to whisper.

'Do what you want, my darling, but do always remember the way you have been brought up. And now, don't you think you could put your dress on properly? Most people have both arms in the sleeves. You only have one.'

She had thought she had finished dressing. She pulled on the dress and went back to her room to add the finishing touches to herself before dinner. Madeline was waiting for her, a worried look on her face, as she had heard the riot.

'Your mother's agreed, love. I can tell by your face.'

Elfie pulled a comb through her untidy hair.

'Yes. She's agreed.'

The door was flung open again and the aunt raged into the room.

'I hope you are pleased with yourself. If your mother doesn't die tonight it will be a miracle. And if she does die, we all know who will be to blame!'

High-coloured, furious, she slammed out again, leaving Elfie in tears, horribly afraid her impetuosity had killed her mother. Suppose she did die. And it would be all her fault.

And to be left with the aunt as her sole guardian was a fate worse than death.

Madeline, herself now angry, held the girl tightly and tried to soothe the stormy sobbing. There was too much emotion being generated all round. They were all suffering from the aftermath of the shock of the sudden death of the master of the house, tempers were rising and feelings were out of hand. The aunt, an emotional woman at the best of times, was feeling the strain of her responsibilities, and she had never approved of her brother-in-law or the way he had brought up his crippled daughter. She considered Elspeth was thoroughly spoiled and needed to be taught her place, and if her mother would not do it, being too weak, then her aunt would.

The aunt had a tremendous sense of the dignity that went with their station in life. It would have been bad enough to have a son of the family working like a groom in a stable, but a girl, working alongside a sergeant, not even an officer and most certainly not a gentleman, a man who would never be allowed any but the tradesmen's entrance to the house, it was unthinkable. She almost choked with fury.

Elspeth, who had spent the day very happily, sure that everyone would approve of her having sold Rory for a good price and found paid work for herself to help the family finances, had travelled through too many extremes of emotion and Madeline had a difficult task in quietening her, but at last the sobs stopped.

'I hate her. I wish she was dead. I wish I was dead. I never do anything right.'

'Hush, love,' Madeline said. 'Wash your face and sponge those eyes in cold water. I'm going to see your mother. Stay here till I come back.'

Elfie did as she was told. Her eyes ached and her head ached and she felt sick and didn't want any dinner. She wanted to go back in time and have her father to talk to. He would have approved of her actions.

Her face washed, she held the flannel to her reddened eyes, but they were too inflamed to remove all traces of tears.

She turned her head as Madeline came back into the room and, smiling happily, ran across to her and hugged her tightly.

'Your mother's sitting up, drinking soup, and she's pleased as Punch with you. Says she's glad you've grown up at last and done what you want to do. She's been worried sick because she knew how unhappy you were.'

Elfie felt as if she had just been given all the King's horses.

'Come on, now, love. Powder your nose, brush your hair, then stick your nose in the air, girl, shoulders back, and down stairs you go and walk straight to your chair like a lady. You've just grown up and it's time everyone knew it.'

By the time Madeline had helped to repair the damages caused by crying, Elfie felt as if she were grown-up. Her mother might be an invalid but she still ruled in her own home and Elfie was her daughter and the aunt did not belong. She stood at the top of the stairs, remembering ballet lessons. Stand up straight, walk as if you have a book on your head, and walk tall.

She went into the dining-room, aware of curious eyes. The family expected her to be chastened. She took her place, and ate her meal, suddenly conscious of the fact that she did not care about her aunt's disapproval. Aunt could storm and she could rail until the stars fell out of the sky, but Elfie was going her own way and, what was more, with her mother's full approval and that was all that mattered.

Nothing more was said. Someone went to vet the stables and talk to Mr Jones, and reported to her mother, who sent for Elfie and told her that he seemed an excellent and responsible man and she could work for him. Elfie never did find out who had gone on her behalf. Several members of the family had been staying, as well as the aunt, until everything was settled. Tiding over, they called it. No one made any further comment.

The next week she started work.

Chapter 12

It was wonderful to escape from the atmosphere at home. She left early, feeling as if she were starting work at dawn, as there was a long way to go and she had to be there by eight. Madeline made sure she was up in time and ate a good breakfast, knowing it would be very hard work. Maybe the craze wouldn't last, not once the thrill of being with horses had gone and the days consisted of long hours of stable work, of mucking out and cleaning tack and all the various odd jobs that had to be done. There was water to be fetched, hay to be put into nets, feeds made up and sick horses to be looked after. Privately Madeline thought her charge was in for a shock. It would be very different from just one pony, almost as a game.

She arrived on time, to find her employer and a tall schoolboy already mucking out. This is Bob, said Mr Jones, and Bob, this is Miss Pollok.

Bob nodded to her, but didn't speak and she was too shy to say anything.

Elfie worked hard until the morning break when Bob was sent on an errand and Sergeant Jones took her into the office, sat her down, and proceeded to talk in a solemn voice. She was a 'young lady' and it was very unusual for a young lady to work in a stable. He expected her to behave like a young lady, no nonsense and no schoolgirl behaviour, she was now grown-up. And if he found her wasting time, loitering, or talking to Bob, she would have to go.

She was totally embarrassed, knowing that some member of the family had been down to talk to Sergeant Jones and made the position very plain indeed. She would always be singled out, be made to feel different. She didn't belong to the family; she felt alien, as she was always letting them

79

down, and now they had made very sure she would not be accepted anywhere else on her own terms either. And she couldn't see any crime in talking to Bob, but she would have to ignore him. She was not going to lose her job.

It was years later that Bob Wilkinson told her he had also been lectured, and much more severely than she, as the Sergeant vowed all sorts of punishment if he committed the crime of talking to the new young lady who was their stable help.

Ted Jones had not been a sergeant for nothing. He supervised his two young helpers as if they were part of the regiment he had once drilled. And he was determined that both of them would become first-class riders. They had to, to work with him. He was a very hard task master, but was always fair.

There was a great deal of work, apart from learning to ride. The stables consisted of four stalls and a loose box, all under the same roof. The stalls were tiled round the mangers, and had corner hayracks and heavy wooden partitions which had brass rings that had to be polished, and white reins on each end. The loose box was beautiful, very large, with wooden partitions on top of which were iron grill rails which separated the horses from one another. Everything had to be immaculate and cleaned each day.

The tack always looked superb, but the metal was steel that rusted and had to be cleaned with hard labour every day; and if it were used it was cleaned again.

The bits, the stirrup irons, the buckles, were cleaned with emery paper and silver sand, and when every speck of rust had vanished, were polished with Silvo or Brasso, depending on the type of metal.

The bridle buckles and the stirrup bars had to shine; and Sergeant Jones had very keen eyes and inspected the work when done. If it did not meet with his approval it had to be done again. He would have no slapdash work in his establishment.

Bob was new to the work, too, and they slaved side-by-side, blamed for using too much water or not enough, and it seemed weeks before either was praised for the leather work. They could not please their master. It was very different from Art School.

Somehow the bits and stirrups seemed to grow rust after they had been done and hung up and a few minutes later would come the barrack-yard bray.

'Take that lot down and do the whole thing again *properly.*'

Mucking out, Elfie also discovered, was not a job: it was an art and it had to be done just so, or else. She was asked to move a pile of straw from one place to another until her employer was satisfied that she was using the pikel with sufficient skill.

The pikels were unusual, sawn off very short and Elfie thought they had been adapted to the size of the stable help, and one day she said so.

'I don't have things for you; only for the horses, and I'm not having my horses stuck in the belly with them things because I can't get decent stable help.'

She was not allowed to have anything to do with the midden for a long time, whether because of her small size, whether it was considered skilled labour, or because he felt muck didn't go with her family status, she didn't know. The midden was a strenuous job; it had to be under cover, absolutely square, regimental square, and was watered once a week. When it got to a certain height, it was shelved. Elfie and Bob were sure that at night when they had gone Sergeant Jones went round with a ruler. (They did manage some communication after a few weeks, although they were always very careful indeed never to be alone together in the stables or to waste time. That he would not have.)

She did not realise that she was no longer the crippled girl. She still had difficulty at times with her legs, but the constant walking and riding were strengthening them and she felt herself normal. The more critical and the mean-minded did notice she walked at times with difficulty, especially at the end of the day when she was tired; and with this job the end of the day found her physically almost wrecked at first. But she was not going to give in.

The meticulous instruction she received from the very correct Sergeant Major Riding Instructor made her realise how little she had known, but she was avid to learn, absorbing knowledge with a determination that surprised her employer.

He had been dubious at first. She was small, she was obviously suffering from some kind of physical disability that might affect her, she came from a family that were against her occupation and had had an upbringing very different to his. She was officer material; he was just an ordinary common man. And Bob was an unknown quantity too. Lads could be silly or difficult or just plain bloody-minded so that Bob might ignore his instructions and take advantage of the girl who was only a child. One thing he did know about was lads and men.

Bob was as avid to learn as Elfie. Neither of them had time to worry about fun or games.

At first Elfie found it difficult to work with so much formality and the constant awareness that she came from different stock. It irritated her. She was human too, not a rare piece of china to be treasured, although she didn't get much treasuring apart from the insistence that the midden wasn't her job. Everything else was.

She learned to school the horses and found that she enjoyed that almost more than anything else she had done so far. She could understand them, sort out the timid and the bold, anticipating naughtiness and preventing it, with a quick eye and an ability, as she learned, to move faster and take on more responsibility.

The stables became better known.

Horses were brought in for schooling and Elfie schooled them. She slept at home, but her life was with the horses; she left before the other members of the family were around, but she was always home in time for dinner, and Madeline had her bath ready and her evening clothes laid out, as servantless or not, with the staff reduced to only two, they always changed at night. Sometimes she longed to lie down and rest as her whole body ached, but the evening had to be endured.

She began teaching children and found she had a flair with them, understanding their difficulties and worries and sometimes their nervousness, as parents sometimes made children learn to ride who were afraid of horses. She had never been afraid but her problems in learning had been worse than most.

She could ease their anxiety and make them laugh.

'Goodness me, you mustn't fall off. It makes the place so untidy. Horses don't like untidiness. It worries them.'

Miss Pollok will take you.

Please, Miss Pollok, would you school the Hamilton's pony for me today? She wished he would treat her as he treated Bob, with easy informality. She felt tolerated but not belonging, as if she were doing them an immense favour and would one day leave and go back to the kind of life she ought to be living.

She and Bob were at last earning approval for their tack cleaning; there were also the rugs to clean; and the horses to strap, and tack had to be repaired. A saddler friend was brought in to teach them how to do this.

The saddles were unpicked and re-padded if they were worn, or if they did not fit the ponies. A badly fitting saddle was uncomfortable for the rider and misery for the horse.

Manes had to be pulled and so did tails, and had to be done right. The horses and ponies had to be clipped and trimmed and often other people brought their horses in for them to be done at the stables. There were different ways of clipping that had different names, and it was a crime to do the wrong one on the wrong type of horse. A terrifying mistake that could not be rectified.

The stable ponies had to be turned out every day as if they were going to a show. They were on parade and were an advertisement for the place, and not one of them must be ill-done. At times both Elfie and Bob wished they could ease up, but both in after years, when Elfie had made her own mark in the world and Bob was working with the Windsor Greys in the Royal Mews, were grateful for the instruction they had had in those early days from a man who sought above all for perfection and who placed the wellbeing of his horses above that of the humans who cared for them.

And Mr Ted himself was always immaculate.

She had been at the stables for some considerable time and was still Miss Pollok, treated with respect by both Bob and her employer. She wished they would relax. She needed companionship, not deference. The break came one sunny day when she could do nothing right. She rode badly, she handled the horse badly — and that was a major crime. Nobody was allowed to handle his horses badly and Sergeant Jones forgot she was Miss Pollok, forgot she came from a very good family, forgot she was a girl and gave her a trouncing that would have been salutary for one of his former recalcitrant privates.

Suddenly he remembered who she was.

'I'm sorry, Miss Pollok,' he said stiffly.

Elfie, amused by the sudden change of attitude, simply grinned at him.

'I asked for it,' she said.

He looked at her, said 'You'll do,' and went off, but next day she had stopped being Miss Pollok and was Polly. She and Bob began to chat, with constant checks from their employer to make sure they were behaving, as they cleaned tack or mixed feeds.

One afternoon when she had been particularly school-mistressy with some of the children, Sergeant Jones grinned at her and said, 'You're a proper Auntie Muriel, aren't you, Polly?'

Auntie Muriel was one of the regular speakers on Children's Hour, a programme that went out daily at five o'clock and had a distinctly avuncular air. When Bob or Mr Jones wanted to tease her after that she was 'Auntie Muriel'. But she was much happier. She belonged at last.

She was riding well and although her legs at times shook and sometimes wobbled, she suddenly realised that neither

84

Bob nor Ted Jones knew why. She was not a cripple to them in any way, and by now she and Bob were treated alike. She had a way with ponies and could adjust to any and soon grew so overconfident that, riding Rory one day, she was bucked off.

That was a heinous sin. Ted Jones added to her mortification as Bob Wilkinson was told to take over the ride; she had to learn to be a more sympathetic rider and to anticipate her horse's behaviour, not to come off like a novice.

Elfie was furious and began to hate Bob. Bob continued to treat her well, perhaps understanding that she felt he had shamed her, but perhaps from an innate gentleness. She did not know then that he too had just lost his father, who had been at sea, and had had to go to work as his mother had been left penniless.

She was still obsessed with herself and her own problems and was unaware of the needs of others, although she was very considerate with the children who came to her for teaching and was beginning to learn to assess their characters and those of the horses she rode. But as yet, people older than herself were difficult to understand.

But now Bob rode her own pony and she wasn't allowed to. She still thought of Rory as hers in spite of the money she had received for him and felt that Bob was being favoured. It wasn't fair.

One day they were sitting in silence on the floor, cleaning tack, both of them cold and both of them miserable. Elfie did not intend to speak to Bob. He only spoke when he had to and called her Miss Pollok again. It had been pouring with rain but by eleven there was a watery sun and the clouds were parting.

'Saddle up,' said Ted Jones. 'We're going out exercising.'

Elfie usually rode a dun. His name was Duke but he was always referred to as the Pig, even in front of clients. He had a neck like india rubber, he napped and he reared. He preferred to put on his worst behaviour in front of an audience, when crossing a road, or out with a ride, which

Elfie thought was probably because he was bored. She could cope with him and never minded his rearing; she sat tight, held on and encouraged him to resume the more normal stance for a horse.

Sergeant Jones by now was known as Mr Ted by his stable help. He was to ride Comet and Bob was on Rory.

Exercising was much better than cleaning the bridles which were all in pieces. Elfie rushed to put one together and saddle up and was ready first.

They went out of the stables, a half-mile ride and then on to the bridle path, trotting sedately at first and then Mr Ted gave the order 'Canter'.

This usually to Rory meant buck, but today he decided to be sober and they settled at a nice steady pace, side-by-side behind Comet.

She was unprepared for the Pig developing a new trick. She was almost unseated as he suddenly went into a series of bucks and then into a bolting gallop. Her nearside rein came away and they were off, racing over the ground at a terrifying rate, totally out of control. They were almost on the main road, a major road with fast traffic. Elfie tried to reach the bridle, got a bump on the nose and then felt nothing but blind panic. A moment later, Bob arrived alongside her, grabbed the Pig's reins and pulled both horses to a halt in real cowboy style.

Mr Ted reached them, out-of-breath and without any colour in his face and stared at them. He had had visions of both being killed.

Elfie had been scared almost witless and was suddenly certain that Mr Ted would sack her if he knew she had been responsible for her own misfortune, as the reins had not been buckled properly. Nor was she going to allow Bob to be even more favoured because he had saved her from a very serious accident, perhaps even from death. If she lost her job everyone at home would say 'I told you so' and she couldn't bear that either.

Fear made her lose her temper and she swore at Bob. He might have put the rein on properly after cleaning the bridle.

It was all his fault. He'd done it on purpose because she was a girl and a better rider than he was anyway.

They ignored her outburst and walked back to the stables in silence. Bob took Rory in to unsaddle him and Mr Ted helped Elfie dismount.

'If Bob hadn't been so marvellously quick-thinking, you might be dead by now,' he said. 'Just think about that, Polly, will you?'

She thought about it, but according to Bob it was twenty years before she learned how to admit she was wrong and apologised, very belatedly indeed, for her dreadful behaviour.

They continued to work side-by-side, and even managed to time their riding accidents so that one was off while the other was able to work. When Elfie was in hospital Bob was her most faithful visitor. He had forgotten his shyness and completely ignored her churlish behaviour on the day that the Pig had bolted. He was the man in his family and had had to grow up fast. Other people took responsibility at the Pollok home and there Elfie still led the life of a leisured daughter, with servants to wait on her. It was a different world and she often felt that she led a double life.

Often they used to hack to the country shows, riding the horses for miles before competing, as horseboxes were rarely used. The animals had to be very fit. Nobody worried about distance; the sport was what mattered.

Rory could jump. He had a very big jump and, when he chose, was magnificent. But he also had a temperament: nobody was ever sure what he would do next. He might refuse to enter the ring; on another day he would take every jump in such a way that he smashed it to firewood. And then he would go like a hero and be in the ribbons. It did not make for consistency but it did make for a great deal of interest. There was no chance of swelled heads with Rory either.

Showjumping was in its infancy. No one ever knew what kind of jumps there would be and the competitors varied from the outstandingly excellent to the frankly terrible.

The Pig was as much of a Pig when jumping as when

riding him, but Mr Ted drove him in a high-wheel gig, a Dalmation dog trotting behind in the style of the old carriage dogs. They gave an outstanding performance and could be relied on usually to win.

Life for Elfie was still rather odd. One night, when they had been working very late, Bob walked halfway home with her as she was nervous in the dark. Mr Ted discovered the fact and Bob was well and truly chided. After that Mr Ted himself walked Elfie home on winter nights, sometimes Bob with them. They stayed at the gate for a brief goodnight and never ever stepped inside.

Elfie went in at the back gate, up the back stairs, leaving boots and gaiters in the kitchen. The family was most suspicious of the goings-on at the stables, never realising the work was so hard and unremitting that no one had time to think of anything else. She bathed and changed into her evening clothes. Her sister was away from home, living in the nurses' home and spending her spare time with her own friends. Her brother was now the head of the family, very conscious of his position and even more conscious of Elfie's uncouth friends and that she, so he said, always stank of horses. Dinner was invariably an ordeal. She felt like a visitor in her own home and what was worse, a visitor who was beneath the family but who they had to endure as some kind of penance visited on them by an unjust God.

Elfie, like the Poor, was always with them, but they did not have to be kind to her.

By the time she was twenty-one her mother was recovering, and up and dressed every day although she retired early to bed. Elfie had, of course, to have a Coming-of-Age party, a dinner and a dance afterwards. Everyone did. The problem was that owing to the very odd life she had led she had no acceptable friends. She asked if she could invite her older riding pupils and Bob and Mr Ted. The request was refused. Certainly not.

A guest list was drawn up and the day arrived; a new evening dress; a beautifully prepared dinner and afterwards the dancing; with a company consisting of people she scarcely knew, who seemed quite alien to her, and some very old family friends, referred to as the fogies.

She found the fogies very kind. Everyone made a fuss of her as it was her night, but she did wish her own friends could have been there. Wistfully, she had asked Bob and Mr Ted if they would at least come to the gate during the evening and see her new dress. They came, perhaps more aware than she realised of the conflict between her two lives, and they stared at her. They had only seen her in breeches.

They had little gifts for her and she had hoped for a comment but she received a surprise. Mr Ted looked at her in complete amazement and then bent and kissed her.

'Just like Cinderella,' he said. 'A fairy princess that can change in seconds to our everyday Polly in her breeches.'

She suddenly remembered her father. 'No matter what other people think, Elfie, you are *you*.'

She had her place, with her friends; with Mr Ted and with Bob who felt as she did about animals, and home no longer mattered. Nor did her brother's gibes. That day, too, made both men aware of the divergence between her work and her home and how unhappy she was at home. Their treatment of her changed. She belonged with them and Mr Ted tried to make up to her for some of her family problems.

He knew she had little in common with anyone at home and that her evenings were spent alone, retiring to her room after the meal where she read or painted or drew. She had illustrated several more children's books. It was a little extra money, but it meant nothing. It was an occupation, a way of passing the endless hours until she could get up and start living again when she went to her work. She never went to parties and she seemed to know nobody apart from him and Bob.

Somehow during the next few months Elfie and Bob became part of his family, in and out of the house with his wife and small children. He teased them and laughed with them and one day, after torrential rain that prevented riding out, the horses were done early.

Everything was damp: the wet horses, the sodden straw,

the tack, and so were the three of them, trudging through the rain mucking out and fetching hay and dry bedding.

'Come on, hurry up,' said Mr Ted, and the three of them set off. 'We're going to the pictures.'

They arrived, macs soaked, collars up to their ears, hats pulled down to shield their faces from the driving rain and went in looking like steaming scarecrows to see *Lilac Time*. None of them had enjoyed a show so much before and for weeks afterwards they laughed at the disgusted looks they had got, the way handkerchiefs were put over delicate sensitive noses and gradually the seats around them cleared. They didn't care.

Nothing lasts. Life changed. It was the 1930s: men were out of work everywhere, prices high, incomes low and times were hard. Mr Ted found he could not afford to pay either of them. The horses cost money; they had to be fed and shod and there were vet bills to pay, and rides were fewer. Elfie worked for nothing, not daring to tell her family. In return she was trained as few riders ever are trained. Mr Ted was determined she should benefit.

By now she was fascinated by racing and wished that women could race. She read all she could and watched all she could and went when she could, and at one meeting an Irishman asked her to ride one of his horses. It was an informal affair where a girl could ride.

She won.

He offered her a wage such as she had never dreamed of to go and work for him. Home by now was impossible; everyone hated her work and said she must give it up and take up art again, or she could perhaps teach it, that would not be so improper. But she knew her drawing was not good enough and competition was fierce and the only thing she could do really well was to ride.

She didn't know what to do.

Take the job, said Mr Ted.

If she did her home life would only worsen. She didn't want to explain to Patsy Murphy, the Irishman, that she led a strange existence, belonging nowhere, torn between two totally different worlds but longing to stay with horses.

She had been offered the chance of a holiday with clients who had become good friends. She would decide afterwards. But she knew that she had to leave Mr Ted.

She couldn't work for nothing any longer.

And she had to do something about her home life which was becoming intolerable.

Meanwhile, she'd think it over, she told Patsy Murphy. And she would let him know.

He had to be content with that.

Chapter 13

Elfie's holiday was the first she had ever had with people like herself. They took her to Newmarket, to a relative who was a racehorse trainer. When they went home Elfie stayed on, enchanted by the racing life. Horse talk, talk of winning, talk of race entries, talk of breeding, talk of jockeys, talk of trainers, talk of owners.

Training; training for the Derby, for the smaller races; talk of racecourses. The horses were all around her: sleek and elegant beauties, each worth a fortune.

At first she was a privileged visitor and heard the owners' viewpoint and the trainers' viewpoint, and as time went on she did not want to go back to Oxton. It was too difficult to change from her main interest during her working hours to the narrow impossibly snobbish atmosphere of her home, an atmosphere that had worried her so much that she had spoken of it to Mr Ted. He had tried to help her cope, but that was far from easy. She did not feel as the family did, that her employer was outside the scope of society, a person to come in at the tradesmen's entrance, a person to whom she very kindly gave her time, as if she were being condescending to him.

The family thought this was a phase and she would grow out of it. They worried in case she married one of these unsuitable people, so beneath her, but that thought never occurred to her. She felt herself a professional horsewoman and she was already developing skills that were to lead her on to a life so remote from that led by her relatives that they never achieved common ground.

The days went by. She couldn't go back. She was living, for the first time in her life, free from the strain of pretending in the evenings, free from the difficult personality conflicts that met her when she returned at night, free from the occasional feeling of guilt, of letting the family down as she worked with the children or took out a ride or mucked out a stable.

Here everyone shared her passion; and they took it for granted that she felt as they did about the horses, the most important creatures in their lives. The lordly aristocrats, cosseted and protected by their attendants; the royalty of the horse world.

Newmarket was the centre of racing. She wanted to make her life there. She wished more and more often that she had been born a boy. She was small and could have been a jockey; she was light and she could ride and would ride better. She could never ride a racehorse past the winning post but she could learn to know the world of racing and asked her hosts to find her a job. It would take her on; where she did not know, but it seemed a step in the right direction.

Her hosts were doubtful. She could only start at the bottom, there was no other way. Did she really want to? Was she sure?

She was positive.

She became a stable lad; a messenger boy; a droppings-shifter and a yard-weeder. She was given one lowly task after another, and week after week she seemed only to watch others with horses; others ride horses; others care for horses, while she did all the odd jobs; toted hay and filled the water buckets and fetched and carried and was at every-one's beck and call.

But she was surrounded by heroes and racing talk and she didn't care that again she had the role of Cinderella. Nobody mocked her at night or said she stank of horses, or called her the stable girl. Although her room was bare and cold and her days were hard and long, she was happy as she had never been happy before. There was no more pretence.

She wanted to ride.

The weeks went by and the need to ride became an obsession, but nobody thought of giving the lowly stable girl a ride.

One winter morning, the string was ready to start. Six-thirty and bitterly cold. Frosty and clear; bringing out the horses, hooded and blanketed; the cosseted kings and queens.

One of the more frisky was bored and naughty and struck out at his unwary attendant, who was too badly hurt to mount.

The horses had to be exercised, all of them, and there wasn't another lad.

Elfie summoned her courage to ask the Head Lad, a charming elderly man, if she might take the injured man's place. He stared at her. A girl, up on one of his precious racehorses.

'I can do it,' Elfie insisted.

The ride had to go out. He glanced at the horses and changed over some of the riders, giving Elfie the quietest mount of the string. She was up, on a real racehorse, going out to the morning gallops. Single file, one after the other, the lads dressed as she was, and all wearing tweed caps, as she also did, as it made her less conspicuous in the yard. They wore them back to front to ride and she hastily changed hers round. She was wearing ordinary trousers and laced-up boots, was riding with racing leathers, which were very short but as she had short legs that made no odds.

She dreamed of galloping on the downs, one furlong, two furlongs. She had never ridden a horse at the gallops. She didn't even know what they were like.

Up on the downs to the waiting trainers. Dismount and walk around. Gallop this one; gallop that one; walk this one. And again. Elfie walked and walked her horse. Nobody asked her to gallop. Or even canter.

She stood by her horse's head, chilly and shivering, as the endless discussions went on. Everyone except the trainers looked bored. After the first exercise gallops, this horse was tried out, then that horse was tried out and then the string turned for home, with Elfie still walking her mount.

So much for her dreams of glory!

The next day she was allowed to ride again, but someone

94

else galloped the horse while she watched and stood by her horse. At least she wasn't cold as her charge was so restless she was kept warm just hanging on.

The rides made one difference as the other lads accepted her as one of them and not some sort of freak. Girls in the 1930s just did not work in stables. She had to accept that, but as she worked with them and talked with them and thought like them and rode with them, they forgot she was a girl. She also dressed like them.

Talking with them taught her more. No one ever talked about anything but horses and racing. Then she was rewarded with her own charge to 'do'. A horse of her own to look after. He was regal, he was handsome and after her ponies he was enormous but Mr Ted had taught her very well indeed and she felt immense pride in turning him out the best groomed of them all.

Everyone had to pass the Head Lad's tests for grooming, strapping and cleaning before they were allowed to ride out. She passed, but there were still no gallops.

She had been looking after 'her' horse for weeks when she did get a canter. Then, later that day, she was asked to ride out with the second string and, to her shame, was bucked off. She wasn't hurt. The horse was easily caught; it was a common enough occurrence and although she was teased nobody cared very much. It had happened to all of them at times.

When she was thrown again she was told to use glue or spit and stick on next time. She loved the bickering and the teasing, and the easy way some of the less-important lads flitted from one job to another. Elfie, being least important of them all, had to do some gardening, sometimes doing the house grounds, sometimes the drives; and when stable lads gardened the garden boys teased them. They told her impossible names for flowers, or chided her for leaving weeds and pulling up the plants.

The place had always to look like a modern film set; every blade of grass regimented and shorn; the lawns billiard table smooth, not a weed in sight. The yards were spotless, the rails white painted as soon as they began to even appear faintly dingy, and everyone worked endlessly to keep up the standard required.

Elfie loved watching the owners: VIPs from all walks of life arriving in large limousines, driven by liveried chauffeurs. Most exciting of all when she did ride out were the days when His Royal Highness Edward, the Prince of Wales, himself, arrived at the gallops to watch his horses, and she could see him — although only at a distance. He loved his horses and was always there at dawn, whatever the weather. He stood in rain, hail or sunshine, his eyes noting every detail of the horse, its ways and its performance.

The other lads told Elfie he was no mean rider himself and she had proof of that one day when she went hunting; her mount that day was an also-ran, a good sort of horse but nothing fancy and, although it went well enough, she was not among the stars. His Highness was, riding hell for leather, never mind the obstacles, right in the front the whole of the way.

Time went by. Other lads went to the races with their horses, but never Elfie. She only rode out with the string when no one else was available. She stayed in the yard, detailed to garden or muck out or fetch and carry while someone else took the horse she regarded as her sole responsibility.

Regretfully she decided that Newmarket held no real future for a girl.

She had been happy with Mr Ted and was homesick, not for her own home but for him and Bob Wilkinson. They had been her only real friends and her only confidants since her father died. There was no one in her family she could talk to; no one who shared her interests or could understand her fascination; no one who approved of her career. It wasn't a career to them. She disgraced them all, letting the side down. It wasn't playing the game.

She looked at the life she ought to be leading, in their eyes: visiting friends with her mother; attending coffee mornings; doing good works; a kind of Lady Bountiful; a committee

96

lady; and then a good marriage, to go on with the same sort of meaningless artificial life.

Why on earth couldn't women do the same jobs as men? They were quite capable of it. It was insane to fetter them with conventions that were already dying; to pretend life was the same as it was when she was born. It wasn't. But her mother and her mother's friends and the family tried to keep up the old ways; and like the dinosaur they would die out and new ways would come. Her father had prophesied that before he died and it was beginning to happen. There were a few girls now working in stables, but they didn't come from her kind of family.

More than ever she wished she had been born a boy, and that she had been born into a much lowlier family. They might have been interested and backed her instead of regarding her as a failure and her work as a social crime.

She remembered the fun she and Bob had had with Mr Ted, becoming almost part of his family, with his wife and little girls to talk to. She remembered too the absurd walks home in the dark and the need to say goodnight under the lamplight at the gate as he wasn't good enough to cross the sacred precinct; as if it had been some sort of secret rendezvous. But Mr Ted was very formal on those walks home, very conscious of his duties to the girl he employed and the promises he had made to her family.

Memories of days with Mr Ted remained for ever inextricably woven in with the old lap at the garden gate, and the last real conversation before running through the garden and in at the back door as she wasn't allowed to use the front door when she was in her stable clothes.

She returned from Newmarket to Oxton. Mr Ted had come on even harder times as the slump was now biting deeply; there was no chance of him paying Elfie. Bob had had to find other employment; he needed money too.

She couldn't manage on air and riding lessons, she had to have paid work. She knew she must have a change, but she did start with Mr Ted again; it was hard to make up her mind as she didn't want to go. She was happy there. She missed

Bob's friendship, although that was to remain with her all her life; both of them married and their children became great friends. Many years later Bob worked again with Elfie; she trained his daughters and whatever happened in their lives, they kept in touch. And they are still in touch, although she is widowed and retired and living in Anglesey and he is back again working in the Royal Mews, and is a widower. Both of them have travelled a long way from the days with Mr Ted.

She took up her belated invitation and joined Patsy Murphy's yard. She felt that she might stand a chance in a smaller outfit, but until she reached it she did not realise how she had gone from one extreme to the other.

Nor at the time did it dawn on her that she was accidentally giving herself the most liberal education possible in the horse world, as she knew the peak of perfection, among the racehorses of her Newmarket days, and now she was to find out how those her relatives so despised really lived.

Newmarket had been an eduction. Murphy's yard was to be an education and a half.

Chapter 14

Life at home did not improve. Murphy's yard was even lower in her family's estimation than Mr Ted's place. She found herself, more than ever, leading a dual life. But her evenings were mostly solitary as she found it was often easier to get home too late to bath and change for the formal family dinner.

She sometimes wondered if the family imagined they did very little work and occupied the hours tumbling in the hay. It was impossible without working with horses to dispel the odd ideas non-horse people had, of fun and rides and romance. It was impossible, too, to convince the family that she wasn't that type of girl, although one or two lads who had tried it on with little Polly found out to their cost that she could handle them as well as she could handle horses. They had soon learned to keep their distance as if they pestered her to any extent beyond that she considered reasonable, they suffered painfully. She no longer had the gentle manners when dealing with bad behaviour; she could take care of herself very capably and neither marriage nor 'carrying on' were on her life plan for a long time. She had other ideas.

She expected always to be accepted as one of the lads, and damn being a girl. She was totally professional in that respect.

At Murphy's she rode daily: she hunted, she schooled, she taught, she showed horses off to clients and she worked.

They all worked.

Out in the early hours before anyone but Madeline was up. Once she was in the stable she ceased to be Elfie. She was Polly to everyone, shortened from her surname.

There were always at least fifteen boxes to muck out and often more. The water taps were as far away as a thoughtless installer could site them, and the heavy old-fashioned water buckets had to be lugged for what felt like miles. Patsy checked the haynets constantly. There was no half-filling them or shaking them out to make them look fuller than they were.

Shaking the hay was easier than today as it was stacked in trusses. The trusses were tied with bale string which was cut at the knot and pulled through, so as not to waste hay caught in the knots and also to make it easier to plait. Ropes were made with several plaits plaited together and also halters had to be made to use for leading out to and from grazing. There were no idle moments; Patsy could find jobs nobody else had ever dreamed of for any lad seen with time to spare on his hands, and Polly was one of the lads. No quarter for her; she wanted to work in stables so she worked.

The loose boxes had to be cleared of cobwebs frequently and there seemed to be a horde of remarkably busy spiders; Elfie still hated spiders. Droppings had to be removed as soon as they were made, and stable and yard had to be kept immaculate.

When they mucked out each horse was quartered, rugs were straightened, feet were picked out and all shoes were checked. A loose shoe, dirty hooves, bad clenches or not properly quartered meant a severe talking-to, with the culprit made to feel thoroughly ashamed of such sloppy work and carelessness. The horses might look rough and shaggy and ill-cared-for when they arrived, but they never stayed that way for longer than it took to detail a lad to take care of the animal and bring it up to stable standard.

Somehow Patsy so inspired his lads that to let him down left them feeling both shame and despondency. They really had let the side down and were determined not to commit that fault again.

It was a good yard with good relationships, everyone working as a team and extra work always shared. Nobody seemed to beef about conditions, although compared with today they were appalling: long hours, very hard work and not much pay. And no labour-saving devices of any kind.

Patsy not only noticed faults, he praised good work and made sure that everyone knew that the work had been well done. He was a tiny man, with a strong Irish brogue, a dark man with eyes that often laughed, a very just man, with a dislike for sharp practices and a way of dealing with it all his own.

He turned his yard to all sorts, to hunting, to schooling, to training, but the dealing fascinated everyone as nobody knew what would come in next. Making a horse was an art and Paddy excelled. He taught his lads that what was needed all the time was patience and confidence as well as an ability to work out what kind of animal you were with; and how to get its trust and how it would respond to training; not all needed the same kind of treatment. Every horse was an individual with a way of its own, and Patsy stressed the fact. It was to stand Elfie in very good stead for the rest of her life.

The cobbled yard had to be hand weeded; never a weed dared show its head. The stalls were scrubbed and the brasswork polished; and when the horses were ready for a ride they were turned about in the stalls, saddled and bridled with the side reins clipped on. All manes were immaculately trimmed and damped down, the tails were pulled or plaited, the hooves oiled, the hides burnished, the tack polished until arms ached and lads were weary but the results were worth every aching minute.

It was worthwhile to gain Patsy's unstinted praise.

The saddle room was up stone steps. It was a huge place with a central heating stove, the saddle racks down one side, the bridles on the other long wall, the bits in a case which had glass doors that also had to shine. There was a well-stocked veterinary cupboard, boxes for the rugs, in which was kept a dart board, although there was not often time to use it.

In one corner were shelves for tinned milk, cocoa, tea and biscuits; and hidden in the boot-cleaning box were packets of five woodbines and matches well wrapped up in old rags and kept a deadly secret. Immense care had to be taken

101

because of fire; straw burned very easily and a blaze would be a disaster.

The place had to be fit for royal inspection at any moment of the day; not just when royalty appeared, not that it ever did, but Patsy wanted to be sure that whoever visited would carry away a first-class impression of the efficiency of his yard.

Elfie, travelling home exhausted, her legs often at times rebellious, her odd walk still noticeable although nobody ever seemed to bother at the yard, would walk in through the back door and drop into a chair in the kitchen until she had recovered enough to go upstairs. After changing for dinner she sat wondering if anyone had the least idea what it was like to lug buckets over icy cobbles, or muck out in driving rain, or struggle with a horse that was only half-broken and had a temper on him like a tropical tornado.

At times she herself wondered if it was worth it, especially during one bad week which started with a horse falling in the ditch. She was beneath him, but luckily did not take his full weight. Hooves flailed, Elfie lay unable to move and several of the other lads struggled to drag him off with ropes without her being more injured than she was; and they didn't know how badly she was injured.

She emerged only slightly bruised but rather shocked and for once they did treat her like a girl and made a fuss of her. She went on working, thankful it was no worse, but ill luck hadn't finished with her. A few days later she was clipping a horse while two lads were working the Wolsey machine, when he lashed out with both barrels and got her in the ribs. She screamed with pain and he followed up with another go at her. The two lads were sure she was laughing, as they themselves were swopping jokes and hadn't noticed the first kick, but they suddenly realised she was crying, not laughing, and lifted her up. It was only then they saw how badly hurt she had been; two ribs were broken and her knee was swelling as they looked at her.

They broke for a 'cuppa', and then one of the two lads decided to clip while Elfie held the horse. He found the blades broken. Patsy, coming in at that point, cursed her for being so careless and blow her injuries, she could go up the granary steps and get more clippers and get on with her work. She had to finish the horse and the lad held it for her, but what with the agony of two broken ribs and a knee that had swollen to almost football dimensions, it was a very badly clipped horse.

She was in pain for weeks but the only sympathy she had was because a horse had fallen on her; being kicked when clipping was entirely her own fault! Patsy, being meticulous in such things, also deducted the cost of the clippers, 7s 6d, (an immense sum in those days), from her wages.

The family could add her numerous injuries to their disapproval. Not every family had the skeleton in the cupboard living at home, or the black sheep sitting down to dinner, but they did. Also you could ship off a male black sheep to make his fortune elsewhere in the world, but not a female one! They never mentioned her unsuitable occupation but tried to pretend that she, with her uncouth friends and uncouth occupation, didn't really exist. At times she wondered if she did exist for them, as she sat alone in her room drawing or reading, wishing it was tomorrow and the day could begin again and she could start living. It was like being put away in a cupboard until she was of use again.

One person who did get to know her a bit too well was her doctor. 'Not you again?' he would say, as she arrived with yet another kick or bad bruise, or swollen finger or other odd injury not suffered by those who had more mundane jobs. She sometimes wondered if her three times a week visits accounted for the fact that hardly any doctors' children ever came for riding lessons. One of the other lads seemed to be as often a victim as she was, while the other lad who did not ride was luckier, but then he couldn't get any falls.

He did suffer badly on one occasion when Patsy's winning grey hunter was being treated for her main fault: she would not carry her tail high. She was a lovely big-fronted mare, with a beautiful crest; and a true show hunter except for that one fault. So Patsy very carefully applied chilli paste under her dock just before entering the ring which made her carry her tail correctly. It was an unorthodox treatment and it needed doing with the utmost skill.

At one of the bigger shows, Patsy was missing just as his class was due to begin. Johnnie, the lad who never rode, decided to be helpful and went in to apply the paste so that the mare would be ready when Patsy arrived as time was getting short.

He went into the box. Elfie was standing nearby, holding another horse which would be in a later class.

The horsebox exploded.

Wood shattered, the horse screamed, Johnnie came down the splintering ramp hell bent for ejection, ejected horizontally, weighing fifteen stone, into Patsy who had just arrived. Both men rolled clear and Morning Glory broke loose, looking more like Morning Gory.

Patsy leaped to his feet and caught her reins.

Glory had had enough. She kicked for fifteen minutes while Patsy hung on to her, determined not to be dislodged, leaping each time a hoof came too near him. Johnnie, as bloody as the horse, was helped to his feet and put in an ambulance where they later found the blood came from the mare. He was found, when he got to hospital, to have a bruised liver, a broken rib and concussion.

The mare was cut, but only needed a few stitches. Patsy had a bit of quick thinking to do to explain the accident as it would never have done to confess to chilli paste. A pulled shoe, he said, got caught in the boards and the horse panicked.

Later, recovering from concussion, Johnnie (who, Elfie now discovered, was actually Patsy's brother) upset the nurses by constantly yelling 'silly bitch', but was forgiven when he was aware enough of what was going on to explain he meant the mare that had put him in his hospital bed. By then he was the darling of the ward and nobody wanted him to leave.

Nobody ever used chilli paste again. At dinner that night

Elfie wondered what the family would say if she told the story. It kept a tiny amused smile on her lips, but she held her tongue. Glory went to Leicester later and point-to-pointed successfully.

Elfie was sent to bring Johnnie home. She was guided to the ward by the strains of 'Danny Boy' and was amused to find him surrounded by cleaners, patients and doctors, all there to see him off, while he shone with his own popularity as he never had in stables where he was very much the boss.

Matron, appearing unexpectedly, was angry.

'This is not a concert hall,' she said.

'No,' said Johnnie 'It isn't that, but what a lovely place to sing, and your smiling face like an angel, Ma'am!'

Elfie saw the reason for his popularity as even Matron smiled.

'I'm sure we all enjoyed it,' she said.

He grinned at her, and looking into her eyes sang 'A little bit of heaven fell out of the sky one day'. Elfie watched the grim mouth soften and the eyes light up and the sour face relax and blush.

It was another side to Johnnie. She had often seen him with a terrified horse, heard him croon to a crying baby, and he was wonderful with the very old and with awkward people, and those who seemed ill-at-ease or sharp and canny and defensive, yet he had never married. 'Never met a woman to equal my horses,' he'd say.

Elfie never quite understood him, but that day in the hospital she was very glad she was lucky enough to work with him. He was once asked to sing in public and his answer was characteristic: 'I'll not be selling God's own gift.'

He was a difficult man to get to know, but later Elfie did know him much better and he was her ally in all kinds of difficult situations at the yard.

It was hard to realise the two men were brothers, they were so different.

Patsy soon recognised Elfie's own gifts and encouraged her talents all the time. She was impatient for progress, although she did not know in what way she could progress. At that time she did not even realise that the future in front of her held a challenge and a new way of life that would lead her on to achieve more of her goals.

Chapter 15

Elfie looked at Dorothy in disbelief. Usually when she looked at the horses that Patsy bought in to resell she felt that God's designs had gone wrong somewhere. He had brought this batch over from Ireland and most of them were rough, shaggy and unkempt, but this dainty mare stood out like a star among them.

She was 15.2 hands high, threequarter bred, and although a pale chestnut, with a lighter mane, she appeared to be the perfect lady's hack. Most people preferred a stronger colour, but Dorothy had quality. She had been groomed and trimmed and had three white socks. She was also shod, which was most unusual.

She stood, eager and alert, reminding Elfie of her race-horse days.

'That's a real money-spinner,' Patsy said happily, not being in business for the good of his buyers. 'Put her in one of the top boxes; rugs, best of attention, the lot.'

Dorothy enjoyed attention. The next day Elfie tried her out in the paddock and a few days later was told to take her out hunting. She had lovely conformation, the most beautiful flowing action and carried two good ends. She went freely, seemed amiable, and would be seen by the right people if they hunted her.

Patsy sent them out with a rich pack with rich members and Dorothy was seen, admired and sold. Elfie, however, had not enjoyed her day. The mare was temperamental and played up constantly, needing a firm hand and a readiness for almost anything in the way of odd behaviour. She jumped and they did land on the other side of every fence, but with considerable discomfort for the rider. Elfie managed to stay aboard, but with all the skill in the world she had one heavy fall, luckily in a remarkably awkward place that had sorted out other riders so neither Elfie nor Dorothy was blamed.

Patsy met them at the end of the hunt and Dorothy did not come back to the yard. Elfie was given a very generous handout, so knew her price had been well above normal.

Three days later Dorothy came back.

Her buyer said she was unsound. Also she reared, jibbed and napped. Patsy wasn't unduly bothered. Wrong owner, insensitive rider — she'd gone all right for Elfie. There were plenty of other customers. The vet came and could find nothing wrong.

'OK,' Patsy said to Elfie. 'Ride her this week. We'll sell her next Saturday to Lady X for eighty-five pounds more. She's a lovely looking mare.'

Dorothy behaved herself most of the time; occasionally Elfie had to deal with rearing and napping, and the mare at times seemed flighty for no reason whatever, and then she would settle to behave like a perfect lady.

Lady X bought her, very happily, and was delighted with her for almost a week.

Then back came Dorothy.

She was sold three times. Three times she was returned.

She reared, she napped, she jibbed. Everyone began to hate her and Elfie dreaded going down to the yard in the morning and being told 'Dorothy's back'.

The vet came again and could find no reason for unsoundness. Patsy tried one of his usual injections; that took time to work, but did work, and then when it wore off she was up to all her tricks again. Then she behaved herself and was sold again.

Again she was back within a couple of weeks. With exactly the same story. Patsy began to give others of his stock in exchange, instead of giving the money back.

Reluctantly, even Patsy agreed that she was a 'wrong'un'. The rest of the yard hated her. She was like a bad penny, forever coming back.

The dealers began to know her and their comments were

108

scathing, sometimes ribald. Patsy's chief rival, Brodrington, started a ridiculing campaign: he had a fund of low tricks and was always belittling 'the Irish yard'. His shady deals spoiled their trade at times and he latched on to Dorothy as proof that Patsy was as lowdown cunning as he.

Patsy was not. If he sold a bad horse he gave the money back and took the horse back or gave a satisfactory replacement, and he was genuinely sure that Dorothy, sold to the right person, would give every success. After all with Elfie she went, at times, so sweetly. She seemed to have a dual personality.

She was so goodlooking too; a credit to the stable until she began to perform. They tried to show her but they never got her into the ring. She gave a memorable display that was talked about for months.

She worked fairly well as an escort horse and those who came to ride begged to ride her; she was so glamorous. But Patsy dared not risk it; he did not want to say why so the story was that she was far too good for schoolwork and to let any rider take her would cause jealousy as she was so much more glamorous than any of their other horses.

They soon discovered that Brodrington's tongue was behind some of Dorothy's returns. He would visit the buyer and tell a long history that exaggerated her faults and the number of times she had been sold. And, of course, he always had the perfect replacement in his stables.

Patsy was a rough diamond. Brodrington, in contrast, appeared to be a gentleman, always perfectly dressed, riding a beautifully schooled wonderfully turned out horse, and his glib tongue told a convincing story that took in many people. But he never took in Patsy, who had his own standards and knew the background of too many of his rival's deals, selling horses that Patsy wouldn't touch.

Dorothy was back in the yard one morning when Brodrington appeared. He had a titled client looking for a beautiful mare. Had Patsy anything suitable? There was nothing in his own yard. Money was no object; he would pay Patsy's price and still be able to make a good profit.

109

Patsy brought out his stock. He dared not bring out Dorothy — she was far too well known. Brodrington began to enjoy himself. This had three left legs. What was that? A milkman's horse? He wouldn't sell that odd-looking freak to a rag and bone man. And where did that come from? Thrown away on a tip?

Everyone listened and raged.

At last he went, saying he might have known that they would only have rubbish, not even fit for the knacker's yard.

Patsy stood in his own yard and watched the man drive off.

He was a lay preacher, which in Patsy's eyes added to the insults, and his lavishly furnished over-decorated small house was ornamented with texts galore. He never sold a horse on Sunday, although he would always oblige and show it — not himself, but paying Patsy or Elfie to do so as he couldn't desecrate the Lord's day but didn't mind a bit if others did in his own service.

If a horse was wanted on a Sunday he paid Elfie to groom it and display it. The cheque was never written on a Sunday and on Monday when the horse actually changed hands, Brodrington was incredulous. Oh no, sir, I am so sorry, you must have misunderstood. I said two hundred pounds, not one hundred and fifty; you must have misheard. Big innocent blue eyes reinforced his absolute honesty and few people ever questioned him. He always got his price.

'All right,' Patsy said. 'I think a taste of his own medicine would do that one a power of good. I've had enough. I don't see why we shouldn't wrap up a parcel for him. And Polly can come and help.'

After lunch they went into the barn, armed, from Elfie's viewpoint, with mystifying parcels, buckets and a hose and scrubbing brush, and Dorothy herself. By the end of the afternoon they had not a wishy-washy chestnut but a beautiful bay mare with black mane and tail. Elfie hosed her down, dried her off and exercised her till she sweated. No sign of colour on the white blanket. She had watched with interest. This was something she had never met before.

110

Patsy rang his rival. He had the most beautiful mare just come into his loose box, which was true as up to then Dorothy had been kept in a stall at the other end of the yard! Brodrington arrived and stared. He made light of her, but Elfie could see he was impressed and he was back an hour later with his client, who fell in love.

Patsy named his price. Elfie thought it outrageous, but it was paid and a few minutes later Brodrington was in earnest consultation with his client, asking her a price that gave him nearly one hundred per cent profit. It was accepted without question.

Later that evening Dorothy went off in a magnificent horsebox.

Within a few weeks she was for sale again. Brodrington accused the groom of being useless with horses; it wasn't his fault and he wouldn't have her back. She was to go to the sale ring.

Patsy had a problem. He didn't want Brodrington to sell her to anyone else as she would revert to her original colour very soon. He decided they had to try once more. Maybe the mare did have possibilities; maybe with the right customer; he was sure that something so attractive had to have a use, have her good points, would settle down with the right home. They just hadn't found it yet.

Elfie was to bid for her, as a girl wanting her first pony so that they got her cheap. They admired her in her stall and Elfie clutched what was supposed to be her savings. Patsy wanted the mare back but he wasn't going to pay a big price for her. And she would revert to chestnut once he got her. She was still bay.

Elfie was dubious until she read the catalogue: 'New Penny, owned by a Lady. Perfect lady's hack. Sold without warranty.' No owner's name, so she wouldn't fetch much anyway, and without warranty meant that she would be sold without reserve and no return, so that she would only go to a mug or to some other dealer. And Elfie didn't see why an innocent should suffer; and if she was going to a dealer then they might as well have her.

111

She became the new owner of the pretty mare, for £14. There had been no other bidders.

Patsy gave her £15 and took her out for a meal. As they left the sale ring Elfie saw Brodrington's expression. He realised he'd been done but he didn't know how he'd been done. He thought he'd done Patsy by selling the mare at double the price he'd paid for her to her Ladyship. Brodrington was mystified. What had gone wrong? He thought even now that Patsy had landed himself with another mare as bad as Dorothy. He was a very puzzled man.

They drove into the yard and the word went round: 'Dorothy's back.'

Slowly she reverted to her wishy-washy colour. She was unsellable till she had. She was used as an escort horse, looking a grubby, peculiar animal. She wasn't happy. And her manners were even worse. Nobody could do a thing with her. But Patsy seemed to have a soft spot for her and he never gave up.

Donnie, the local milkman, was a Scotsman with a large dairy herd who often helped with strapping. His hackney, Rooney, looked spectacular in the milk float and won all the firsts in Tradesmen's Turnouts at the local shows.

Donnie came in sad one night. Rooney was getting past it. He wanted another showy replacement, but there was nothing in the yard.

Except Dorothy!

'She looks right,' Donnie said. Patsy looked at Elfie.

The next day she and one of the lads were told to try the mare in harness just in case. The harness was old and patched, used for breaking only. Dorothy hated the collar and when the crupper was put on she kicked. Once everything was fastened she settled to almost amiability and Elfie drove her on long reins round the paddock with Patsy yelling at her.

'Don't let yer reins slack or you'll get two in the belly.'

Within a month Dorothy was driving freely in the breaking cart, although she wasn't too sure about her blinkers as she had never worn those before.

Everyone became excited by her progress and Dorothy was put into the float. They set her well forward, thinking they would be safer from kicking if she felt like that. The lad led her and Elfie drove. She waved the whip well above blinker level and off went Dorothy, smoothly and freely.

Dorothy cantered, but then settled down and the lad climbed in with Elfie. Round the field, circling. Driving between the jump stands, Dorothy handling as if that was what she'd been meant for. On her last lap Elfie realised Donnie had arrived and was watching. He was extra interested as they'd filled the float with bottles to get her used to the noise and she was behaving as if she had always been driven in a milk float.

He came over and took the reins.

They watched the mare circle the field, with Donnie driving her faultlessly. Dorothy was happy and at home, round and round, figure of eight, stand, four square, ears pricked, eyes bright, an absolute raver! They couldn't take their eyes off her.

'She's mine,' Donnie said. 'She's perfect.'

'Leopards don't change their spots,' Patsy said. 'A fortnight's trial. And then you can have her. No money yet.'

Being honest he told Donnie her history and Donnie laughed.

A fortnight later Patsy asked for twenty-five pounds for the mare and was given forty.

Within the year she was the most spectacular animal in the Tradesmen's Turnouts, beautifully groomed, mane and tail gleaming, dazzling everyone with a new brass-mounted harness, and the show float revarnished. She assumed great dignity and a spectacular action, straight from the knee, 'throw 'em out' with a slight hesitation, seeming to float. No one had seen anything to touch her. She never let Donnie down. He won everything he entered with her. Her whole character changed and she even delighted in the daily round with the milkfloat.

Best of all was the day that Brodrington watched Donnie win with her. His face was a study and Patsy, not wanting to push home an advantage, invited the man for a drink. He refused, very rudely.

'Oh,' said Patsy, 'Sorry, old boy. I saw you biting your nails and I should have thought of the gastric ulcers swelling. I shouldn't have tempted ye. Another time maybe.'

Oddly, after that Brodrington was more civil.

And Patsy, every time he saw Dorothy and Donnie made the same remark:

'I told you there was a place for her and she only needed understanding.'

He sold Elfie Dorothy's saddle for eight pounds and she had it for the next thirty years, as a memento of a remarkable mare that had had a place, but they had had many defeats before they found it, and of the man who recognised that she did have good qualities when everyone else thought she was hopeless.

All the same the yard was relieved when Dorothy was finally sold and the staff all voiced their feelings with the same remark:

'I hope we never get another one like her!'

Chapter 16

Life at Patsy's was unbelievably varied. Elfie might be out hunting, sent with different packs, to get experience, to show off horses, and more and more to add to her own skills. She went over different terrain and always on different horses, jumping, galloping, and all the time learning.

She might be jumping, or teaching, or schooling, or nursing a sick horse, or making a young horse.

She was saving up for her own horse, and then she'd see. A good horse, not an also-ran; it was an ideal, a goal, a determination that kept her going when she ached all over, when injuries hurt, when the family were more than usually scornful and when their snobbery goaded her beyond endurance.

Patsy knew her quality and sometimes felt she should have been born a boy. She had what it took to get on in the horse world and she began to earn his respect. She made mistakes; she was young and inexperienced, but he never remembered that she walked awkwardly, never treated her any differently to the rest of the yard. She might be a girl, but she would be reprimanded as if she were a lad.

And more and more of his clients were borrowing her and tipping her. Every tip went into the fund for her own horse. Over the trotting poles with a pony brought to be schooled; over the cavalletti; guiding it, talking to it, imitating Patsy whose soft horseman's voice gave so much confidence.

Easy, boy, easy there. Easy little lad, easy there.

Steady, whoa there, steady now, steady.

Confidence — it was the top and bottom of it all. Knowing what the horse could do and jollying it to do that little bit better. Over a small jump, splendid lad, splendid, now try this one and over you go. Throw your heart in front of it, the

115

old horsemen said, send your heart over before your horse. Give it confidence, help it all you can, teach it all you can, so that it responds to you with total trust and will work its own heart out for you.

They came in week after week; easy rides and villains; rodeo horses and gentle horses; spooky horses, shying at shadows, shying at imaginary tigers in the bushes, shying at a noise or a paper bag or a child suddenly shouting in the distance. Learn to anticipate, read your horse.

She found two Kipling verses that to her typified all she was learning, and they remained as part of her life. The first was only a small piece, a tiny scrap from *The Conversion of Aurelian McGoggin*, but once she had read it it stuck in her mind:

> *Ride with an idle whip, ride with an unused heel,*
> *But once in a way, there will come a day,*
> *When the colt must be taught to feel,*
> *The lash that falls and the curb that galls and the sting of*
> *   rowelled steel.*

There were colts like that, and there were others that had to be gentled and coaxed and taught to master their fears.

Reading at night, tired out from her day's work, in the silence of her solitary room, she added to her knowledge, thought over her experiences, counted the far-too-slowly-growing fund towards buying her own ambition. And she dreamed of racing, a dream that could never come true.

On a night that followed the kind of day that nobody should live through, when a horse had died and the yard was plunged into gloom, she came across another Kipling piece from *Thrown Away*:

> *And some are sulky, while some will plunge,*
> *(So ho! Stand still, you!)*
> *Some you must gentle and some you must lunge.*
> *(There! There! Who wants to kill you?)*
> *Some — there are losses in every trade —*
> *Will break their hearts ere bitted and made,*

Will fight like fiends as the rope cuts hard,
And die dumb mad in the breaking yard.

Luckily there weren't many that couldn't be made. Make a horse, not break a horse, Patsy said it over and over.

More and more often now, 'his' Polly was asked for to help school a brash youngster, or teach the children. Her own past experiences had made her understanding, although she rarely remembered her awkward legs now. She could use them to ride and she was forever on them, walking, lugging hay and pushing wheelbarrows, heaving up sacks of feed; stronger than she realised, with powerful arms and shoulders and a will with a horse and way with a horse that was all her own.

She was now competing in the small shows, although very unsuccessfully. In some she rode for other people; the tips were always treasured and saved but she loved it so much she would have done it for nothing, although it was better not to say so; and as others took tips, it was better for her to or she might be thought to be stealing their rides.

One memorable day she was booked to ride in what was known then as a leaping event (only the yard called it 'lepping'), but would now be called showjumping. It was in Liverpool and she was riding a mare called Marie Louise.

Dressed in her best breeches, with highly polished brown lace-up boots into which she had put a great deal of work, she also wore buckskin buttoned gaiters and topped her jacket with a bowler, which almost invariably fell off. This happened so often that she was teased about it. She felt very proud and very elegant as she rode out on her immaculate mount; the tack had also had the full treatment. She aimed for absolute perfection when she was on show.

It was a lovely day with brilliant sunshine, and the mare was a sweet ride. She rode her to get the feel of her and then asked how she liked to be ridden; what sort was she and how did she like to go, which fences did she prefer and which was it she needed to watch? Elfie felt really professional; today

117

she was Polly, the rider, a different person to the one who went home at night; she suddenly felt as if she really were two different people. She certainly wasn't Elfie the cripple any more.

It was nerve-racking waiting for her turn; with an uneasy feeling of excitement rising in her, knowing she had to master it or it would travel down the reins to the mare. At last she was called into the collecting ring. Now there was no way out unless she was tossed off ignominiously while waiting and badly injured or the yard caught fire and they sent for her in a mighty hurry or some disaster happened in the family.

She felt dithery, not in command at all. She was about to make a fool of herself and mess up everything and nobody would ever ask her to ride for them again. Her tongue felt dry and she felt sick. She walked round the ring; would her turn never come? A canter; and then a walk. There was one horse with three faults, one horse with only one, if she could keep it down to four she could come third. If only ...

Imagine being third! She had never been placed at all in all the shows she had competed in; always there had been those fatal mistakes which meant nothing at the end of it. Just one of those who also ran.

The last horse before her; and five down.

Number 13.

The significance of that number suddenly dawned on her. Unlucky thirteen, Unlucky Polly; she felt much more like Elfie, despised and always an afterthought.

Into the ring; in front of the crowd, all eyes on her, including those of the other competitors and of the owner of Marie Louise. She had to do her best for him. Try to forget them all. Concentrate. They had had to wait too long; the mare was bored and silly; Marie Louise played up and fly jumped; she was over eager as she had been waiting so long. She was tossing her head and feeling frisky.

Polly let her flow on and then tried to steady her. No hope. She was gassing up, fizzy as they come, and all that her rider

118

could do was to sit as quietly as she could, deep breaths, steady herself, calm, calm, calm.

Clear, and clear and clear again; jump after jump after jump going like a veteran; and then there was the water. Nobody had cleared that. Elfie accelerated, let the mare have her head, raced towards the water jump and over it, faultlessly, the only one to take the jump without coming to grief.

There was a roar from the crowd. Elfie blinked, not quite knowing what to make of the noise and then came the voice from the tannoy.

'Number 13. Clear round.'

She had been the last to go.

'Number 13. Marie Louise. *First*.'

She couldn't believe it. She was dreaming; she would wake up any minute. She must have fallen off and hit her head and now she was in the ambulance. She had ridden in hundreds of shows by now and never ever been even in the first four. A real novice, and she had won!

She couldn't wait to get out of the ring; she wanted to dance, to leap, to shout, to hug everyone. She had won, she had won, she had won. Deep breath and control her face and line up; collect the coveted rosette; lead the lap of honour knowing that she was a credit to the horse and the horse a credit to her; head high, bowler still on. She, Elspeth Pollok, had won.

She wished her father could have seen her; she had flown to the moon and back, and was still riding on air. If she never won again the agony of learning to walk and ride would have been worth this moment. She was sure that everyone was admiring her and her mare.

She was waiting for her employer, for the day's congratulations, for the people milling round them as they came out of the ring. She leaned forward and whispered to the mare as she patted her.

'Wait for it, old girl. They'll be round you like flies in a minute, just see you behave, they'll pet you and fuss you and we'll both feel like heroes.'

Out they came and the crowd surged forward, but as she was about to dismount a voice rose high above all the congratulations:

'She may fancy herself for having won, but just you watch as she gets off. She can't even walk properly let alone ride.'

The bubbles burst and the champagne feeling went flat. She hadn't done anything to be proud of; she was not even an ordinary rider; she was still a freak, to be sneered at and mocked. Elfie the cripple; the daftie in her awful cloche hat and veil. She wasn't going to get down and let everyone see how badly she walked.

Her friends had not heard the words, they had crowded round, wanting to hug her. The mare's owner wanted to toast her; their faces were as sunny as the day and they couldn't understand the tears in her eyes. They were over the moon and completely bewildered by her behaviour.

'Polly, what on earth is wrong? You did splendidly. Come on, get off.'

'Not till I reach the horsebox. I'll get off behind it, not here. Please.' She could only sob. The jolt to remembered misery and a disability she thought everybody had forgotten had been too great. In one moment she had gone from one extreme of feeling to the other, from triumph to total despair. The shock was the greater because it had been so unexpected.

'You can't get off there,' the mare's owner said. 'You have to go for the cup.' Everyone was bewildered.

She refused to dismount. They led her behind the horse-boxes and friends crowded round, worried, anxiously trying to find out what had upset her. Finally she managed to stop sobbing and explain, at which point Patsy, now furious, rolled up his sleeves and wanted to try and find the culprit, and fight him or even her! Elfie wasn't sure; the voice had seared her, but she couldn't identify its owner.

By then the story of the cause of her misery had gone round the showground with the speed that such tales always do, and one of Elfie's other friends came over with a bottle of champagne and poured a glass for her. They jollied her and cheered her, and persuaded her to hold her head high and damn the critics and go and collect her cup and join in the Grand Parade.

'It's only jealousy, Poll,' one of the lads said.

The Grand Parade proved an ordeal in a totally different way. The Lord Mayor was to present the cup; cameras were ready, Elfie was posed in the saddle, the group of VIPs around her, when up went Marie Louise, waving her fore-legs in the air, totally overfaced by the crowds, the noise and all the attention. Everyone ran. The cup came off the plinth. Elfie clung on, but in the end was forced to dismount and accept the cup on foot.

Marie Louise had no intention of being mounted again. There was nothing for it; Elfie took her own bit between her teeth metaphorically. She thanked the Lord Mayor, took Marie Louise's reins and walked beside the mare as she danced, hanging on hard, the cup safely under her arm, as she tried to keep upright, never mind walk.

OK, she thought, laugh if you want to, I don't care. I may be lame but I'll never be proud again, or afraid of what people say. Just wait. I'll show them all.

She had almost reached the crowd when Patsy and Marie Louise's owner ran up to her, and hoisted her aboard, Patsy giving her a leg up, a tremendous air about him, playing to the gallery, making himself the centre of attraction for the moment.

They paused and faced the crowd. Elfie held the cup high and the mare's owner led her out and the crowd went wild. Marie Louise, not wishing to be left out of the action, bucked her way to the horsebox, showing off.

Both men made very sure the rest of the day was a day to remember and that the spite was forgotten. It never would be totally forgotten. Elfie was to remember it all her life, and it was to keep her feet on the ground and prevent any over-confidence or cockiness; but for that day she did forget. And, being forewarned, the jibe never hurt so much again.

That night also remained in her memory, as they travelled across the Mersey, Liverpool made romantic by the lights on

121

the water. She was still in charge of Marie Louise, but the mare was sleepy and stood quietly, and Elfie, alone at last, watching the reflections, half asleep herself, went over and over in her mind the highlights of a wonderful day.

Chapter 17

'New pony for you to school,' Patsy said one morning.

'I've had a phone call from Mrs Faversham Bromley-Browne with an E. Mustn't forget the E, it's most important. Miss Faversham Bromley-Browne has a very expensive pony that cost her mother a fortune; and Fairfield Silver Moonlight is letting them down when she is shown. We have to work a miracle, my girl. And miracles don't come that easy. Also we have to show respect to the little girl and call her Miss Faversham Bromley-Browne — with an E and don't you forget it, Polly. This one could be tricky.'

The yard watched the Daimler draw in and the poker-faced chauffeur open the door for the be-ringed, be-furred, perfumed and beautifully made-up, extremely large and daunting lady who descended. Her accent matched her name. Miss Pierce would have loved her as 'refainment' seeped from every pore. Patsy, when she went, backed out of the royal presence; his Irish brogue had been remarkably overdone, whether in private amusement or plain panic nobody was sure.

Polly and the lads lurked just inside one of the stable doors, unable quite to believe in any of it.

'The pony is fabulous,' the lady said, 'She *hes* to be, considering the praice I paid for her. But judges are so ignorant and can't appreciate a good pony. May daughtah hasn't even been placed and she is very upset.'

'Oh, gawd,' said Johnnie, as the entourage drove away, 'a glass-case pony and no Christian name; Miss Bromley Davenport-Browne, dear, put your heels down. Go to it, Polly.'

The pony arrived the next day, accompanied by her groom, who got out of the horsebox, looked at the

123

assembled staff of the yard who couldn't wait to see what was arriving and said, to their total astonishment, 'There *is* a pony under it all.'

Red-faced, he led out a hood, several rugs on top of one another, knee pads, hock boots, tail bandages over a stocking, cotton wool from elbow to ground level, and underneath it a mean-looking grey pony that was the essence of misery and stood forlorn, not even looking at her new surroundings.

When all the gear was removed she was good looking. She had brought her own saddle which proved perfect for Elfie who, as the smallest and lightest in the stables, had been detailed to school her. She was already in a panic. Mrs Faversham Bromley-Browne with an E was absolutely terrifying.

The rugs were too good to leave at the yard; the pony's second-best equipment was in a trunk. This was unloaded and off went groom and horsebox and the staff delved into the trunk with some hilarity, finding also a night rug, a detailed diet sheet, on which were doses of tonics, things to be added to her feed, times she was fed, how much to give her, which days to dose what, and the instruction sheet was signed Cecilia Faversham Bromley-Browne, with the E underlined.

'So we know it's authentic,' Patsy said thoughtfully as he pinned it up over Fairfield Silver Moonlight's stall. 'And we'll call her Silver; can't come out with that mouthful every time we talk about her.'

Elfie started on the pony. She was perfectly schooled with a lovely mouth, but her action was incredible — a shuffle behind and a Knees Up Mother Brown in front. That hackney action ruined her for the show-ring and would have to be cured, which was a tall order. Elfie looked at the shoes when she got back to the yard. They were lovely shoes, but light as a feather.

Walk her; try to extend her stride; rein back.

Silver didn't want to know, but three days with Elfie at least got the rein back. She was such a beastly ride that Elfie decided to use long reins and school her on the ground. Sitting on her back was like being on a ship in a choppy sea and her hind legs and forelegs seemed to belong to different animals. Elfie had never ridden a camel but she felt that Silver could have knocked spots off any camel ever born.

The pony's owner arrived a week later expecting a miracle. That hadn't happened but after walking round the little mare she did comment that her condition was excellent and that the stable girl rode quite well considering. Elfie wasn't sure what the 'considering' meant; for a stable girl? She thought of the family and grinned to herself. She was also amused because she could not be addressed directly; Patsy had to act as interpreter between his client and this common creature who worked with horses.

Elfie was too busy considering how to get the best out of the pony to worry too much about Mrs FBB with an E.

The barn was being repaired and one morning, riding out, the men had left a big box of nails and washers in her way. She got down and moved it, a remarkably heavy operation, and rode on to the field.

The little mare was no longer cosseted and over-dressed; now she felt frisky. But although she was lively she was well-mannered and, what was more, she was beginning to enjoy herself; until that happened there was no hope of any improvement. Elfie galloped Silver flat out and she loved every moment and ended with a little playful buck, the first sign that she could act up in any way. She had been a very down-in-the-mouth pony to start with.

Back they went to the trot. Elfie hoped the gallop might have improved her action but not a bit of it; along she minced, knees up in the air, short-stepping all the way. This was useless and Elfie decided to call it a day. She walked the mare to cool her, thinking and thinking. There must be *some* way.

As they passed the barn she remembered the weight of the box of washers.

Weight!

Into the stall, mare rugged up and bandaged for the night

—although not as many rugs as she had had on when she arrived.

Elfie collected two linen saddlecloths and half a bucket of washers and went to the saddle room, where she sat stitching washers galore onto each with mane thread. It was tiresome and tedious and took hours, but she stayed till it was finished and went home very late indeed. Before she went she returned to the mare and wrapped her up in the weighted cloths.

Next day she asked Patsy if the mare could be shod heavily in front, very heavily. He stared at her, astounded, but asked no questions and called the blacksmith.

'If you've a good idea, it's all yours, even if it is mad,' he said, and made no other comment. Elfie did come up with some rather clever brainwaves at times and seemed to have ideas that no one else had. Elfie then insisted, to everyone's astonishment, that the mare was rested for five days and not ridden at all.

On the sixth day Mrs FBB with an E rang to ask if she could see her and view progress, if any. That was annoying as they weren't ready and progress didn't come overnight, but there was no help for it, so it was off with the heavy shoes and the mare was left unshod. Her mane was plaited so that she looked pretty again and no longer workmanlike.

Mrs FBB with an E was early. A frantic all-hands-on-deck got the bandages off and the weighted cloths on, although the lad helping was horrified. 'You aren't using those?' 'Shut up,' Elfie said. 'And don't ask questions. Let's see what happens.'

Damp all four legs and ruffle them up in case they showed as overbandaged and hope the lady's eagle eye did not notice anything unusual. It wasn't exactly orthodox but something had to be done if they were to get results and it wouldn't harm the pony in any way at all.

Elfie, desperately anxious as this was a very lucrative job for Patsy and if they got results would bring in more work for them all, was almost sick with anxiety by now. She walked Silver into the paddock and walked around casually until she was on the far side, when she broke into a trot. The mare immediately extended for the first time; she felt very different, although Elfie couldn't see what had happened. She was still trotting when Mrs FBB with an E and Patsy arrived.

Elfie passed the gate and saw Patsy with a face-splitting grin and his thumb in the air, and Mrs FBB with an E standing for once quite speechless. Elfie was so elated that she gave a small display: figure of eight, flying changes, one from a walk, and then a gallop and a reinback. A perfect halt, right in front of them.

'Wonderful, wonderful.' Mrs FBB with an E was ecstatic.

'Yes, an improvement, but a long way to go,' Patsy said, and winked at Elfie.

'Can I go now?' she asked.

'In a minute,' said Mrs FBB with an E, delving into an enormous handbag.

Ten shillings towards my horse, Elfie thought, hopeful, and a moment later almost fell off Silver as she was given a five pound note, an unheard-of tip for the early 1930s.

She was finishing up for the night when Patsy came to talk to her.

'Miracle,' he said. 'A real daisy-cutter, a real London pony now. You've done it. What did you do?'

Elfie told him. 'She won't know and the pony can't tell.' she said, 'but it may not last.'

They couldn't keep re-shoeing so an extra row of washers went round the coronet in three layers; those bandages were a godsend.

Then came the message they all dreaded: Liverpool Show in two weeks time. Silver had her original shoes put back and was hacked to wear them thin. Then came the sixty-dollar question: did she travel weighted? Did they leave them at home or put them on and take them off before they got to the showground? On the ground, Elfie said and lost her nerve so they stopped on a quiet stretch of road and un-bandaged her, both semi-hysterical with laughter. The weighted cloths had been rolled in old rugs and shoved under the hay in the horsebox, later to be hidden beneath the driver's seat.

They met Felicity, otherwise known as Miss FBB with an E, but she proved to be a delightful child in spite of her mother, and after a short schooling went into the ring and not only won her class but her first championship too, so her mother was ecstatic. Another £5 note found its way into Elfie's fund, while Patsy was given a bottle of champagne.

Elfie was right, it didn't last, three more shows and then back to her natural action and no more wins. Back to the yard for more schooling.

'I can't,' Elfie said.

'Nonsense, of course you can. I always said you had a touch of the Irish in you.'

The miracle was repeated and this time she lasted for four shows before she reverted. She obviously needed to be kept weighted, so that when the weights came off she responded as Elfie had hoped.

'Patsy, I'm not doing it again,' Elfie said.

'And no more you need, Polly. I've an idea meself this time. One that would solve our problem for ever.'

When Mrs FBB with an E appeared once more he smiled at her and suggested they finish the season with the mare and then consider another function for her.

'She's not going to maintain her improvement and you can't keep sending her back,' he said. 'So why not let her go to a stallion and have a foal and I'll find you a pony with a much better future.'

A successful search brought Golden Gleam and a very satisfied Mrs FBB with an E, who by then had added several more fivers to Elfie's hoard, as Gleam was an all-out winner and consistently splendid.

'Thank God that's settled,' Patsy said, when the mare was safely delivered of a foal and everyone was happy. 'My nerves won't stand for another season of Fairfield Silver Moonlight, I can tell you; or for that matter, another of Mrs FBB with E.'

Elfie grinned at him. Her nerves wouldn't stand it either as

128

she had spent the whole season with butterflies in her tummy knowing full well that her treatment would not produce anything but a temporary change and not at all sure just how long they could go on trying and getting nowhere. Poor Silver looked lovely but just hadn't got the movement that it took to get her places; and it was a very good job that Patsy had come up with an answer.

He often did have an answer, but his answer for one particular horse proved pretty disastrous for Elfie.

Patsy couldn't bear a horse that couldn't jump. He taught the new ones free in a lane; the used horses were jumped over everything, while Patsy drove them all with his voice and his 'long Tom', which was a very snaky lash that worked like magic with a sticky jumper.

Among the many horses always coming in for sale was a horse registered as Autumn Bower. The name did not lend itself to any abbreviation so Loppy Lugs he became. He wasn't much of a jumper, but he was a nice horse and since there was a big demand for hunters he had to learn.

Elfie rode him and Patsy schooled. Poor Loppy Lugs was fine over low poles and wornout gorse fences, but he'd never make a show jumper. Patsy watched him, commenting all the time and Elfie soaked up information, learning something new daily.

One day Patsy decided to try a different procedure and when Elfie was in the saddle, he looked up and said, 'He's had time and time over, and not a lot to show.'

'He's more confident and not so sluggish,' Elfie said, defending her mount.

'Well, Polly. I've been thinking and we're not going about this right. He's learned to leave the floor. No bother. So he's got to face up to other fences and once he finds he can do them the battle might be won. Let's go down to the Flats and try him with a few hedges there.' The common was a favourite training place for the hunters. Off they went with several helpers, all anxious to see what happened.

Over a low hedge and out the horse ran nearly knocking down one of the lads.

Canter and try again. 'Now,' yelled Patsy and cracked his whip, and, with some hesitation, they reached the other side safely. It was good firm landing and Elfie's whip was at the ready with two cracks to remind Loppy and he began to take hold.

'Back again,' said Patsy's voice and over he went, easy. Everyone was delighted; they all shared in the yard's success. Two more hedges and then a few more and only two stops. Patsy was dancing, unable to keep still, so pleased with the results of their efforts. His idea was working. As always when excited his brogue became more and more evident.

'That's fine, Polly my girl. Now for a bigger hedge and a ditch and let's see what he does.'

The take-off was bad, sloping to a shallow overgrown ditch and the ground was slippery. Everyone lined up, ready to egg the horse on and Patsy was nearest with his persuader.

Three refusals and Patsy's language became lurid.

Elfie was sweating as much as the horse. It was very hard work. She took off her jacket and handed it to one of the watchers. She was also tired and wanted the thing over; a couple of good flicks as a reminder from her to wake up the horse, she thought, whip ready again, and started a few feet away from the ditch to give him time to accelerate.

Loppy skidded to a halt.

He sank to his haunches on the slippery mud so that Patsy's well-aimed whip, instead of catching the horse, caught Elfie. Loppy struggled frantically to his feet and the whip almost pulled her out of the saddle.

By then Loppy was up and away, Patsy was dancing and swearing in blind fury at what he felt was his own clumsiness and Elfie had no time to think. She was in pain and by now determined that the horse would get over, but needing help from the watchers she yelled, 'Give him *hell*' and turned. Whips cracked, men shouted, Patsy cracked his whip again, very much more carefully, and Elfie, expecting another slide, slipped her feet out of the irons, ready to jump. She turned the horse, who went like a bat out of hell; she

130

hooked him back early, reins in one hand and whip flying.

He soared over like a bird.

Elfie, delighted, jogged to the gate, expecting praise and happy faces. Instead she found everyone trying to soothe Patsy.

'He's doing his nut about you,' she was told. 'He's terribly upset. Put your jacket on and get in the car; well, not on. Put it round you.'

She stared at Johnnie.

'Come on, Polly. I'll take the horse. You're bleeding like a stuck pig.'

She hadn't even realised it but with time to think she discovered her back hurt like hell and she felt rather more exhausted than usual. Back at the yard Mrs Murphy was sent for to give first aid. She took one look at Elfie and another at Patsy and for the first and only time in her life said, 'Take him to the pub.'

Up to the saddle room and strip off while Mrs Murphy fetched water, cotton wool, gauze and bandages, and then looked at the damage.

'Oh my God,' she said. 'He has done it this time. You need a doctor.'

No doctor. It had to be kept quiet. It was an accident. Patsy hadn't known the horse was going to slip and if there was a doctor called in all kinds of accusations might be brought. Patsy had intended to hit the horse, not her. 'If you get a doctor my family will get to know and they already take a dim view of my work. It's pretty difficult at home as it is, so let's keep it quiet.'

There was a deep cut across her back. In the end Mrs Murphy stripped Elfie off and stopped the bleeding by hosing her down like a horse. It was cold but it eased the pain. She was dried off and smeared with a whole jar of boracic ointment, then covered in gauze, cotton wool and bandages; and then her shirt proved too dirty and bloody to go on. Elfie took one look at it and shoved it in the stove.

Mrs Murphy wrapped her in a horse blanket, told her to rest and vanished.

131

She returned so long afterwards that by the time she came, the lads had plied Elfie with hot strong sweet tea, laced with whisky. Elfie managed to look presentable enough to help clear up and then back came Mrs Murphy with a brown paper parcel. Inside was a brand new beautiful primrose-coloured lambswool polo-neck sweater.

'Where did that come from?'

'Patsy,' his wife said. 'He's so upset you can have the moon and the stars if you want them. It's a present from me, my love.'

'Is Patsy all right?' Elfie asked.

'Come and see. They're all worried stiff about you. But don't you dare forgive him too easily; he needs teaching a lesson, the witless oaf.'

Downstairs everyone was round Loppy's stall; Loppy was eating hay, quite unconcerned. Patsy took one look at Elfie and burst into tears.

'That's the whisky,' his wife said.

'I heard that,' Patsy said. 'I heard ye and it's not the drink. I'm thinking she has to ride for Major Fawcett on Thursday and after today she'll not be able to ride. And he wants her, and she'll not be fit.'

Elfie yelled at him.

'I'll come back as usual tomorrow, Patsy Murphy. I'll ride for Major Fawcett and *I hate you*.' She managed to avoid catching Mrs Murphy's glance. Severe pain completed the act and she really lost her temper.

She made a grand exit, carrying her jacket, leaving two hours early, refusing all offers of a lift, full of self-pity and rage. She came to her senses at the bus stop.

She had two hours to wait for her bus!

As she stood there considering that losing one's temper didn't really pay, even if it was justified, two of the lads from the yard arrived in an old car. They took her off to a café for tea and waited with her for the bus, knowing she would never dare mention the incident at home and there would be no sympathy there nor comfort for her injuries.

By the time the bus came they were laughing, and when

she got on the bus promised, 'Wait till tomorrow, we'll make it a good 'un.' It needed to be as by now she knew she was in for one hell of a painful night.

There was no comfort at home, but by day Mrs Murphy treated her like an invalid, and she loved everybody except Patsy, although she rode the Bishop for Major Fawcett. It was a remarkably painful experience but she rode very well and the horse was sold straightaway.

Patsy tried to make friends again and give her her usual rake-off, but she refused it, although she wanted that too for her hoard. She walked in at the yard next day. She was met by Mrs Murphy who gave her double the usual tip.

'Patsy can pay for his sins,' she said.

The trouble was, thought Elfie that night on the bus journey home, that you had to learn everything the hard way; and some things were so silly. She wouldn't make friends yet, but Patsy hadn't meant to hurt her, and she wouldn't leave him. And she did have a very pretty new jersey as a result. And double the amount she had expected towards her own horse.

One thing, life was never dull!

Chapter 18

Elfie learned. She taught, she hacked, she schooled, she hunted, she jumped, she competed and she rode without fear, whatever the horse, always aware that her long-ago dreams had come true. Sometimes, at home, back in her room on her own, the child she had been was so vividly in her mind that she almost expected Nanny to come in with cocoa and turn out the light and her father to come up and kiss her and sing to her, and to find when she tried to walk that her legs did not work; it was not reality, but just a wonderful dream.

And then the bruises would ache and she would look at her workworn hands and think of the day's work, and in spite of loneliness in the long evenings, elation seized her. She, Elfie, had made it all come true. Ask and it shall be given. You are what you are, her father had said. Only you can make things happen. She didn't know if she believed in an afterlife; she wasn't even sure if she was religious at all, but she wished passionately at times that her father was somewhere where he could know what had happened to her and be pleased that his little Elfie had done what she wanted to do and was spending her days in long lovely canters among the clouds. Had it really all happened just because Ned had lifted her up on to Nancy? Nancy's plait was still in her drawer of small treasures.

The work was hard; in winter it was sometimes terrible, especially when snow and ice and bitter winds punished them all; the horses were so varied, some were hateful, some were vicious, some were pure delight; all were horses and she could always find a way with them, unless they were quite mad, and there were one or two of those too.

Patsy was a love; and Patsy could be a demon if the work

were ill-done. Elfie was never sure whether fear of Patsy's tongue or fear of letting him down drove her, but at times she was more afraid of him than of the things he asked her to do. He would set a target way beyond her capability or the horse's capability and there was no arguing. If Patsy said jump, then the horse jumped and so did its rider.

Patsy often wished Polly had been a boy; she was a wizard, and he could have made her a leading jockey. If only. No use wishing. He set her tests. He was fascinated by her ability to pick up his thoughts and ideas, and sometimes to add to them, so that the results she achieved were far better than he had expected.

Patsy's brother Johnnie often came back from Ireland bringing a new batch of horses. He was as different from Patsy as a Shetland from a Shire. Patsy was a tiny, light and quickthinking, impatient man who wanted everything quicker than yesterday. Johnnie was massive, as heavy as the Irish hunters he brought across.

Johnnie was in at the beginning of the next stage of Elfie's career. He had come over with a load of horses that included a big 16.3 'Clyde-built' gelding supposed to have worked on a farm but rejected as far too lively. He was a solid, very energetic horse with a considerable resemblance to a Shire and there must have been some in his breeding. Elfie and the other groom decided to clip him out, hog his mane and pull his tail after he was broken to riding. The result was a very showy heavyweight hunter, and when they tried him at jumping, he adored it.

The days with Johnnie were brightened by his lovely tenor voice, so out of character with his enormous size and strength, singing Irish songs as he mucked out, but so shy he never could look Elfie in the eyes. He had never married. Elfie doubted if he could even stay in the same room as a girl on her own, let alone ask her out or get to know her.

In one of the end boxes was the stable dud: dark brown, threequarter bred, too small for adults, too big for children, couldn't jump a piece of straw, had a rotten temperament so was useless for hacking and everyone was sick to death of him. He was neither use nor ornament and in his box he was a pest; he stirred up his bedding, pawed and fretted and kicked over the water buckets. If he could get himself into difficulties, he did, and had more ways of doing so than most other horses put together. Nobody wanted to buy him so he was put in the bottom stall. Everyone called him Knock On.

When Johnnie was there Elfie always rushed her mucking out to work alongside him and persuade him to sing her 'The mountains of Mourne', which he did beautifully, and if he was in a good mood would add 'When Irish eyes are smiling'. He sang as he worked, moving down the stalls and when he got on to Knock On he'd give him a push over with the handle of the pikel, stopping his singing long enough to say 'Knock over' and then carrying on with his song. Knockover seemed a remarkably appropriate name for this horse as he pushed over everyone who tried to groom or feed him.

One morning nothing would persuade Johnnie to sing. He was so glum Elfie was puzzled and asked what was wrong.

'I'm worrit,' Johnnie said. He went on mucking out, attacking the soiled straw as if it had done him some personal injury. Elfie watched him in astonishment as he was rarely put out in any way.

Finally he sidled up to Elfie, still not looking at her, and whispered.

'I'll have to tell ye. Though I shouldn't.'

This was more and more surprising. 'I won't tell,' Elfie said.

'Well then, Patsy is saying he is goin' to build up the big wall, solid, nailed, five foot six inches and get you to ride Huntsman without telling ye about the nailing and the height. He said you'd be frightened if you knew; we're all frightened. It's wicked. You and the horse'll both be killed.'

Huntsman was the big Shire hunter. Elfie was terrified but she wasn't going to say so.

'Oh, that's all right,' Elfie said, trying to get as much confidence as she could in her voice, 'He's jumping the full course very well and very much in control.'

Johnnie wasn't comforted. He muttered, 'He's a crazy man,' and went on working, not a song in him.

Patsy came into the yard with a man named Kelly. It was evidently to be a formal day. Elfie's knees were knocking and she felt sick. Patsy said nothing but his usual, 'Good morning, you lazy lot,' and she went up the granary steps to the saddle room, and began a marathon cleaning, rubbing away her fears. If she had everything undone ... She undid every buckle; every bridle, every stirrup, every girth, determined to shine the tiniest scrap of leather and be so busy that Patsy wouldn't dare interrupt her. Also all the tack would be out of action.

She was sure she would be occupied all day.

But after half an hour Patsy was yelling at her.

'Miss Pollok, down wid ye and saddle up Knock and Schoolgirl. You and Fred are off to the beach to gallop.'

She had no choice. Fine, she thought, it's only the beach and Johnnie has the wind up over nothing.

She was on Schoolgirl as Knock On was considered too strong and unruly for her; why, she couldn't think as she rode so many misfits and nappy horses; he must be quite exceptional and she longed to have a go on him. The beach was plenty long enough if the horses were kept right. Down the hill, through the town, on to the sand. All ready to start walk, trot, and away!

But there, sitting in the car, were Patsy and Mr Kelly.

'Back,' Patsy shouted. 'Swop horses. I want to try Polly on Knock and see what six stone does instead of eleven.'

Her moment had come and Elfie mounted, excited because she was riding Knock at last and this was real promotion; to be trusted with the stable terror.

Up on his back, with Fred on Schoolgirl beside her; a gentle walk, and then, without warning, without command, without the least premonition of trouble, Knock took off, and she was hell bent for election. Schoolgirl was fast and Elfie had raced her but this was incredible; Schoolgirl was miles behind and they were along the beach at full pelt. At the end of two and a half miles Elfie tried to pull up. She

137

might as well have tried to jump the moon. She tried to turn in a circle, but he was having none of her and off he went over rocks, through a gully of water, soaking both of them, and then Elfie was really worried.

With tears of fury and frustration now streaming down her face she gave him the bells of Shannon, using her whip with all the strength she could summon determined to make him gallop even faster if that was what he really wanted and also determined to master the bridle and damn everybody. They were still flying, the wind adding to her tears as it seared her face.

The horse turned and raced back to the slipway and Elfie pulled up, somehow aware that miracles did occasionally happen.

'Me lovely darlin'' Patsy yelled, although Elfie wasn't sure whether he meant her or the horse. They must have been quite a sight, the pair of them as they sped along. Elfie sat with all the stuffing knocked out of her, and the horse, still restless, walked in smaller and smaller circles and she was sure he would be off again and this time she wouldn't hold him at all.

Fred reached them, white-faced. He had followed all the way, sure he would have to pick up the pieces, expecting at any moment to see Elfie hurled to the ground and the horse come to grief as he raced for the rocks.

'You all right?' Fred asked on the long walk home.

Elfie managed to laugh and lie like a hero. 'I enjoyed it,' she said. Maybe it wasn't much of a lie as once it was all over it was exciting to remember. Patsy was already back at the yard and he added a ten shilling note to her hoard.

She was so astonished she nearly fell off her horse.

'Now,' said Patsy. 'I'll tell ye what this is about. You're riding Knock On in the next race meeting.'

'Girls can't ride,' Elfie said stupified.

'Whose talking about girls riding? Come on, Johnnie Graham me lad, get off that horse, and think about flapping.'

Flapping! It wasn't legitimate racing, but it was for boys and men only and suppose someone found out? She didn't

138

know whether she was excited or scared silly, but she felt ten miles high, full of self-confidence, and didn't give a damn for anyone. She was John Graham! In the tack room, eating sandwiches and drinking tea they talked over the morning, and Elfie recounted her wild ride which got wilder every time she told it, and thought she had finished for the day with thrills.

She was wrong.

There was a yell from the yard. 'Pollok.'

It was the kind of yell that had to be obeyed fast.

Down to the yard again to find Patsy with Mr Kelly who she now recognised as one of the local public house land-lords and with them was a very smart big man wearing city pinstripes and a bowler.

Huntsman was saddled, bridled and standing with the irons ready and as Elfie looked at them she realised they were short and set for her. Her lunch very nearly came back as she remembered Johnnie's warning; and Johnnie still looked as if he had all the cares of the place on his shoulders.

Johnnie gave her a leg up, and leaning against the horse whispered to her.

'It's wicked, that's what it is. Wicked. I'll kill him this night.'

Which didn't help at all.

Out to the jumping paddock. The enormous wall, painted to look like red bricks. Slowly towards it thinking she mustn't show fright; she mustn't be sick, and also realising she was now afraid of Patsy's long Tom. She had to go or she might feel that again by accident!

The practice jump was only broken-down gorse so she asked if she could take one of the other fences for practice.

'Do whatever you like,' said three voices in unison.

Like go home, she wondered.

She jumped the fence, steamed Huntsman up, more by sheer terror than skill, and started the course. He was fighting fit, in tremendous form and ready to go. Over the gate with a foot to spare and turn to the wall and push him on, steady him, steady him, hook him back, hell, she was too late; and give him the whip and yell 'Hup!' and throw herself out of the saddle cursing the day she'd hogged him as there was no mane to hang on to. Six stone of her to lift him, and up he rose like a stag, up and up but not high enough; too late and she tried to look back, but she was high, high, higher than she thought and the ground was one hell of a long way down.

She was back in the saddle. Then she realised she was over, they had done it, they were over that monstrous wall and heaven was here and now and she felt terrific. She felt drunk. She wasn't finished yet. She pushed him on and over the spread and then saw the biggest triple she had ever seen in her life and she hadn't been warned. So what, she found herself thinking, the poles can roll and the lathes can fly and all I can do is fall and it doesn't matter, I've done that before, time and again. This time she motored on and Huntsman stood back and flew. Round to the gate, pull up and wait. Everyone was chattering; it sounded like the parrot house at the zoo. Nobody said a word to Elfie, so feeling they might at least have given her some praise, she rode back to the yard where Fred and Johnnie took her horse and gave her their most fervent congratulations, the more vociferous because they had both been worried sick.

They sat her in the manger, did all her work and treated her as if she were made of glass and so fragile a move might break her; while she sat riding on clouds, too excited to return to earth.

Patsy had vanished but returned two hours late, very merry; he was never drunk, although at times he found it useful to pretend because it was easier to drive a hard bargain if people thought he didn't know what he was doing.

He hugged Elfie and presented her with a pound note and a bottle of Guinness — something she had never seen before. She didn't drink at all, and the family drank wine.

'Drink it down,' Patsy said. 'It'll do you good.'

'I enjoyed jumping Huntsman,' Elfie said. 'I really did.'

'Not as much as us,' said Patsy. 'You jumped like a bird; it was worth a crate of Guinness and we've a photo of the real jump to prove it; ye'll get one too!'

'Not the wall,' everyone said. 'We decided he'd put a foot through that or demolish it; it was the triple that bothered us, nailed up good and proper with the uprights and wings staked like croquet hoops.'

'You gave it an inferiority complex,' said Bowler Hat. He went on, 'You had feet to spare, fore, aft and atop. I've bought the best jumper in the country.'

It was then that she realised Huntsman was sold; they opened her bottle of Guinness and persuaded her to take her first drink. She didn't know if she was drunk with excitement, with success, or with her first taste of drink, but later she lay in her room, too tired to read or draw, every muscle aching, and went over and over the events of her day.

I can walk and I can ride and jump, Elfie thought as she drifted towards sleep. They all say Poor Elfie, the girl who can't walk properly. They don't know anything. Lucky Elfie. None of them will ever know the kind of thrill I had today; twice.

Poor family. Their lives were so dull.

Chapter 19

It was only gradually that reality hit her. Patsy had to be joking. Admittedly flapping races were not recognised by any authority and were looked down on by the elite, but they were for men only; they were tremendous fun; and girls never rode in any kind of races.

'Do you mean it?' Elfie asked, when she had time to speak to Patsy next day. 'What about the rules?'

'Rules were meant to be broken,' Patsy said. Who's to know? Half the people who come here think you're a boy and about sixteen at that. Look at you; little scrap of nothing, short hair like a boy, you ride better than most boys I know, you do the work of a stable lad and do it well, so you're a lad, Pollok, from today on. Don't forget it. One thing though, they're a rough lot and you have to be prepared for anything, but I'm all for you. Got that?'

She'd got it. She was John Graham and she had to remember it.

At night, she lay in bed remembering little Elfie who wanted to be a jockey. They'd all laughed her to scorn, but not her father. He'd accepted it as a possibility. She knew now he had not been sincere, he had been encouraging a child he may well have felt had no future, but for all that he had given her hope and now it was going to be true. Maybe not Ascot or Epsom, but racing was racing, up on a horse whether you did it on the village green or on one of the fancy courses where the nobs went. A horse was a horse was a horse.

During the next few days she veered from elation to panic. She had not done all that well on Knock On on his own on the beach, and now she would be in company: experienced men on much better horses, men used to racing and she was not, and she wasn't a man either. She felt small and very in-experienced, and then confidence would rise again as she remembered how she had ridden Huntsman. She had not realised at the time that she was showing him off to a would-be buyer.

If she rode well she might get plenty of rides as flapping was a craze and anyone who had a horse tended to enter a race, and there might be a chance to ride for other people. In her saner moments she knew she was fantasising, but it was fun to dream and if nobody had dreams there'd be no successes either. If only she had been a boy!

Meanwhile life went on, horses to exercise and groom and muck to remove. Tons of it.

The day came at last. The inevitable beginning to any event involving horses: Knock On to box, and as usual being as awkward as any horse could. The drive to the course, and no problem there as there was no weighing in and no changing room. Horseboxes substituted for everything — and more than everything as Elfie was to find out later when she got more than she bargained for.

Dressed in grey trousers, a blue jersey and a silk cap, heart in her mouth and half sick with excitement and fright, remembering she was a boy and not a girl, up she went in the most motley line-up anybody had ever seen.

Large horses and small horses, rough horses and tough horses, half-mad horses and bad horses, and riders of all standards, but *all* men except Elfie in her disguise. They were lined up every which way, some facing forwards, some backwards, horses circling, rearing, prancing, riders yelling at their mounts, tugging on the reins, with the crowd leaping out of the way and any rider at any minute likely to take off for South Africa or somewhere equally distant.

Down to the start, led by a well-known heavyweight boxer; glory indeed, but Knock On, true to form, had played the idiot till the leading rein was off. If only he'd behave now. If only she could keep her seat, among the thundering crowd.

A yell of 'They're off,' and they were away, with Elfie

143

praying that the words wouldn't come true and she wouldn't come off. She had more to lose than anyone as if she were injured her disguise would be penetrated and that would be the end of a remarkably short career.

Round the first circuit, round the second circuit, up to the third bend and here Knock On decided the race was a bore. There was a duckpond, filled with stinking stagnant slime. It was to the side of the racecourse, but he didn't care; he liked water. The big rangy horse set his jaw, refused to answer to the rein and took off *through* the water.

He decided he was a duck.

Elfie could only hang on. Coming off would be worse. The water was thick and murky and goodness knew if she could even keep her feet if she landed in it, and she didn't fancy going under that stinking weed.

The crowd yelled its delight as a green slimy horse bearing a green slimy mud-covered rider emerged from the pond. Elfie was far from happy; her day was over.

Knock On, as always totally unpredictable decided his wasn't and that he would join the race again.

There were horses in front of him. It was an insult. He went into overdrive and Elfie found herself once more clinging for her life, with the reins quite useless as he overtook one horse after another, passed an exceptionally unpleasant and unshaven character she had christened Wild Willie, who lived up to his name, lashed at her with his whip and swore at her, and Knock On passed the winning post first and went on, down the course again.

She pulled up at last, and slid off. Shivering with cold; stinking mud all over her, slimy and wet with a slimy stinking horse, she met Patsy who looked at her, completely poker-faced and merely said in a mild voice, 'Go and get changed.'

No word about her win. Surely they'd won? There'd been nobody near them when they passed the post.

She crept into the horsebox. What did she change into? A moment later the door opened and someone threw in a jersey, trousers and wellingtons that could only belong to a fat man in a circus. But at least they were dry and didn't stink of mud, even if they weren't too clean. She scrubbed with rags and she scrubbed with rubbers, and got the jersey over her head just in time before the door slammed open. In marched Wild Willie, the whole unshaven dirty lump of him, looked at her with an evil grin and proceeded to relieve himself in the straw. For a moment she thought he had realised she was a girl and this was his way of insulting her as thoroughly as he could. Then it dawned on her that he was simply insulting the rider that had beaten him by using Knock On's box for his own bodily needs. It was only later she discovered that the horseboxes were used by the men; after all the horses had already soaked the straw pretty thoroughly and a bit more made no odds. But they did use their own boxes, not other people's.

It was then that she realised being 'John Graham' was going to have problems. She was in her early twenties and up to joining the yard had led a remarkably sheltered life. Nobody ever performed physical functions in front of other people and she had never even seen her brothers undressed. Willie was also a violent man, as she had realised when his whip lashed at her as she passed, and if he realised she was a girl she couldn't imagine what might not happen. She stood in her soaked trousers, glad at least that she hadn't started to take them off, and shivered with fright and embarrassment as well as some shock; she couldn't say a thing without giving the game away, so she just waited, clutching her dry clothes and praying for him to go.

Luckily he never guessed the truth.

'Going to stand there all day in your wet breeks?' he asked. He grinned. 'I'd try something you can manage next time if I were you. Like a baby donkey.'

He went out, swaggering and pleased with his own wit. At last she was going to be able to change, but Wild Willie hadn't finished yet. He turned in the doorway and grinned at her.

'There's an inquiry, so don't think you've won, you little runt!'

An inquiry sounded very official and most important. Elfie was too miserable and cold to care very much whether she had won or lost by now; she knew the horse was a fool and had no future anyway. And it was very doubtful whether she had either. She found some binder twine and managed to tie the trousers round her waist, and looking like a dwarf in giant's clothing came out of the horsebox, still cold and shivery and not at all sure how Patsy was going to welcome her.

Feeling like Puss In Boots, almost unable to walk in the vast wellingtons, she found herself grabbed by Patsy and shoved into the driver's seat of the horsebox.

'Never mind the inquiry, somebody saw the way he put on speed after his little adventure in the slime.' Patsy grinned up at her, 'and I've sold him for a fortune, and there's a ginormous tip for his jockey too, but watch yerself now.'

She needed to. The inquiry was still going on; those who'd backed Knock On wanted their money; the bookies wouldn't part with it and fights were breaking out all round the horseboxes, bookies were taking to their heels and rough men were trying to beat them up for bilking. It was pandemonium. There was still no decision about the winner when they left with an empty horsebox as Knock On was departing for his new home and Patsy was determined to spend some of the money in his pocket and celebrate, which meant that his girl jockey would be left outside in the box— he didn't take her into pubs.

He did bring her a ginger ale laced with brandy to warm her up and told her to doss down in horse blankets in the box. She thought of Wild Willie and his dirty habits and chose her spot very carefully, and did go to sleep. She woke up when they reached the yard to hear Patsy, fairly merry, ordering a taxi to take her all the way home.

A taxi; her first win, or was it a win? She found she didn't care; she would never ever have to ride Knock On again.

She arrived at the yard next morning to find Patsy grinning at her.

'We won, me clever Polly. What do you think of that?'

She grinned at him and found that she made remarkably light work of all the heavy jobs.

'John Graham will ride again,' Patsy promised.

'Yes, but not on Knock On,' Elfie said, with relief, totally unaware of what the future might hold. That horse hadn't finished with her yet.

Fortunately, she couldn't read the future.

Chapter 20

Elfie was no longer leading a double life. She was leading a treble life. The family knew where she worked, and they were deeply ashamed of her. The acquaintances and relatives of the family pitied them; that extraordinary daughter. She always was odd, of course, a cripple, you remember? Those years of helplessness obviously affected her brain. So unfortunate. Elfie knew what her mother's smug friends said; her brother took care to tell her. Other people's daughters were successful, smart, sophisticated, leading sane lives, going to dances and doing good works, working for the Poor, for the underprivileged, very well aware of their place in society. They made good marriages.

It was their plea to her for a more sensible choice of occupation. Surely she had got all that nonsense about horses out of her head by now. She had been so talented: she could paint and perhaps make her name as an artist. My daughter the artist; our sister the artist. As it was no one could ever refer to her as our sister the stable hand.

The bright tongues wagged; the smart phrases were exchanged; the laughter and the sneers; her mother had to endure them all, but she did not tell Elfie. The rest of the family did.

Nobody understood. How could she tell them? How could she explain that she was only whole when she was with horses; that she understood them; that she had more than a talent with them; and that she belonged, knowing instinctively things that were right. She should have grown up in a Newmarket household where racehorses were a way of life; instead she was born into the wrong kind of home, but she saw no reason why she should stay with that sort of restriction, which amounted to imprisonment, when freedom was

148

hers for the taking. Prisons were not only for the criminal, there were homes that imprisoned almost more successfully by restricting the lives of those within them to a routine that was so deadly it almost killed with boredom. Perhaps if her mother had had some absorbing interest she wouldn't be ill. If Elfie didn't, she felt she would be ill too. What was the point of those years of struggle, of learning to walk and learning to ride, if the exercise took her nowhere?

There were times, at home, when she almost gave in to them; it would be so much easier to live with them if she conformed, but she knew that if she did so she would relapse into a bitter and perhaps very twisted old maid, hating the life she had been forced to live. She could not envisage marrying and fitting into the daily round her mother knew. It would stifle her; it would be a long purgatory leading only to death at the end of a life that had meant nothing.

It was a difficult freedom. She never spoke of her home at the yard, although everyone was aware it was not a happy place for her. Polly and Elfie were two different people. Elfie was quiet, withdrawn, remote, unable to talk to anyone, Polly was excited, alive and full of suggestions for improving a horse, for making the most of a horse, for changing the habits of a pony, for curing a stable vice, or teaching a youngster to jump and enjoy jumping.

Patsy took great care of her; he was aware most of the time he did have a girl in his charge and he made sure everyone behaved when Polly was there. She learned to swear, but only mildly; their language was colourful and sometimes trite and full of stable talk and riding clichés, which were more expressive than normal words, but nobody used the worst language when Polly was around. If a word slipped out, the culprit was given the rough side of Patsy's tongue in private when his stable girl was busy elsewhere.

Many of those visiting the yard thought she was a boy. She was devoid of feminine ways; not for her the fluttering lashes and coyness and the flirtations of her generation. She hadn't time; she had a vocation, although she herself would

149

never have seen it that way. She had been born to work with horses, and she was not going to throw away her chances. Some time the world had to recognise that women could do as well as men in most fields and this was one of them.

She wore boys' breeches and shirt, and polo-necked jerseys or a jacket and a cap; she wore her hair short. She was tiny, so small that most of the yard visitors thought her only fourteen or fifteen, a mere boy in fact. Nobody disillusioned them. When strangers were around she was Pollok. It protected her as well. Nobody bothered about a boy of fifteen; they might well have bothered had they realised she was a girl and looked at her twice. Dressed up as Elfie, no one would ever have mistaken her for a boy.

Now she had a third identity. Already the phone was ringing at the yard. Who was the new youngster riding? Was he available again? John Graham? He could ride, and ride well; a star dawning. As John Graham, she would be mixing with doubtful characters; the flapping races were rough and the riders were rough; the bookies were rough and the men who came to bet were very rough indeed. The horses were rough and the courses were tough.

The sport was unrecognised, with few rules and it was far more exciting than the top races where everything came under scrutiny. If the family ever found out about John Graham there would be the very devil to pay. Madeline was the only person who knew anything about her adventures. Madeline looked after her when she was too badly injured to ride; a broken collar bone as the result of one wild race was the first of her racing injuries.

It came a few weeks after her triumph on Knock On. She was on a horse she had never ridden before, saw a chance and took it at speed and came off with speed. It taught her to ride with more calculation, not to take absurd risks, to estimate her chances and if they were unfavourable, not to rush her fences. It came early enough to prevent her successes from going to her head. It was also disappointing as the horse was a lovely ride and they had been in with more than a chance.

'Teach you a lesson, Polly,' Patsy said when she turned up strapped and with an arm in a sling. 'And just remember, when you stop learning, you're dead. You never know it all. Don't underestimate your elders either; experience counts and there is many a race that was won by the older man and his older horse; both of them knowing what it was about while the young ones had stars in their eyes and rode hell for leather, no sense in their silly young heads.'

She explained her broken collar bone as a fall off a new horse she was schooling. Nobody was interested enough to make further enquiries. It was just Elfie and her stupid occupation again. She sat at their table, ate with them, watched them and wondered how they could stand the sameness of their lives.

Was the wildest thrill in her brother's life running along a platform for a nearly missed train? A good week at the rope factory? An extra specially nice meal or a bottle of rare wine? Surely he wanted more than that? And her mother, often ill now, a weary woman who seemed to have no major interests in her own life. And the aunt who sometimes visited and whose main pleasure seemed to lie in exercising her acid tongue on other people, scoring off them.

The everyday conversation was so repetitive; it always seemed to be of the difficulties of getting good servants; criticisms about the way the world was going from bad to worse; the peccadilloes of the grocer or the butcher; the meat was tough or hadn't been hung long enough, or was overcooked or undercooked and the sauce had lacked savour. The high price of everything. Both her mother and her aunt remembered days before the war of 1914-18 and how little things had cost. The kitchen maid had felt rich on fourteen pounds a year, and she had worked for her money, up at four in the morning to get tea for all the household, the copper to light and fill, the grate to blacklead, the breakfasts to prepare. Girls didn't know they were born now.

Elfie listened, thinking of the early mornings in the winter, hay to lug and buckets to fill, and stall after stall to be mucked out. She knew she was born all right.

The aunt swept her finger along the wooden surfaces and inspected it sourly; these girls never dusted properly; there was dust on the sideboard at the back and they didn't clean the corners. Elfie thought of Patsy's tack inspection; the aunt would have appreciated his devotion to detail if she could ever have demeaned herself to actually talk to such a person.

Wearing silk stockings and pretty shoes and a carefully chosen dress, Elfie wondered if Patsy would have recognised her. Her voice was different, her manners were different; she felt sometimes like a ghost of her real self, sitting there, a changeling, an alien visitor, dropping in to see how the other half lived.

It was a relief to squat in the tack room, eating sandwiches and drinking hot and rather revolting coffee, and listen to Johnnie singing his Irish songs and Patsy telling a long and entertaining story about the last horse sale and how he found a bargain by pretending he had discovered it was lame.

Within months John Graham was becoming better known. She had regular rides for a butcher, for a scrap merchant, for three highly individual Irish priests who owned two ponies between them and enjoyed their racing enormously, and for a vet. The vet soon became an adopted uncle — Uncle Warwick Fowle.

The family might just have approved of him. His greatest treasure was an engraved gold stock pin in the shape of a hunting horn which had been given to him by King George V himself. Elfie inherited it when he died, and treasured it as much as had its owner. Warwick Fowle, rather oddly, combined his veterinary duties with the directorship of a funeral firm that used Cleveland Bays instead of the more usual black horses.

Some years later the Cleveland Bays were also to come to Elfie, who kept them in her stables, schooled them to be marvellous jumpers and hired them out to clients for hunting, which was a remarkable change of occupation for them. They thrived on it. They provided her with a considerable income. Warwick Fowle also owned a lovely hackney mare, which Elfie often drove and showed.

His racing pony was a delight: a lovely ride, without any temperament; she was a consistent animal, a straight winner or loser, according to the competition and she was left to Elfie to care for and ride, without any instructions of any kind. The pony was with her so much and she rode her so often (always as John Graham) that she regarded Jay as her own.

The Irish priests were also a delight. They loved their ponies and were frequent visitors at the stables, with one or the other of them seeming almost always to be there, with help and advice for training. They were very appreciative of their young jockey, who they knew only as John; they treated Elfie like a schoolboy, with generosity and teasing and considerable kindness, sure they were helping a future star to gain experience. John Graham showed enormous promise.

Halfway through the season everyone seemed to change horses. Those they had were not fast enough, or not showy enough or did not win enough, and the Irish priests were no exception; they wanted a winner.

Elfie gained more rides as owners who bought new ponies kept her and those who bought ponies she had ridden regularly asked her to stay with them as she knew them; and soon she was very busy indeed.

The Irish priests, without too much money to spend, risked their savings on a pony named Milkman because he had up to then been owned by a dairy. They thought he looked too 'breedy' for pulling a milkfloat and saw the chance of a profit on the sale. John Graham was duly booked to ride him, as yet unseen, at a meeting in South Wales.

The pony, a very dark brown, came in a hired horsebox that got lost and was late for the meeting, which was far from a good beginning as it meant everyone was flustered. Elfie had met his driver briefly at the Presbytery, but not yet been introduced and now she was introduced to Brother Paul.

Brother Paul appeared to be extremely shy, and he was not one of the three owners. He helped valiantly with tack,

153

with rolling bandages and with holding the pony, as there was a terrific rush to get him ready in time for the race.

Elfie wanted to try him but there was very little time; she jumped into the saddle and gave him one short sprint. Speed, yes, but he'd never been on a racecourse and how would he make out? Also would a milkfloat pony race at all? He was a total unknown.

It was time to go down to the start. Elfie walked Milkman to settle him. Brother Paul joined them and she asked for orders, and then realised that up to now he had helped but had not said one single word. He looked at her with an agonised expression that baffled her and held the bridle, and then as he began to speak she realised what was wrong.

'F-F-F-Father B-B-B-rown s-s-s-aid y-y-you m-m-must s-s-s-s-s. . . .'

His ordeal was interrupted by the starter and they were away, with Elfie wondering what she was to s-s-s. It seemed unlikely she was being asked to pull him up, or rather 'stop' him, as they always wanted a straight race; send him on seemed more likely. Settle him? Soothe him?

No more time to wonder as he was into his stride and going a great gallop. Elfie had no thought other than on riding him and keeping her place. The pony was a lovely ride, so she forgot Brother Paul and carried on.

There was the inevitable thrill of speed; the necessity to work out who was where and how to gain a better position; the estimation of distance; the need to control her mount, not to overface him at the start, to coax him to the winning post and if necessary get that last spurt out of him that would take him into the lead.

There was so much to think about. She knew nothing about this horse. Was he a pony that needed others in front of him for his best efforts or did he need to be out in front of them all, leading the field all the way? She had to find out and store the memory for next time.

Round the last bend and straight for home. No whip needed; he was fit and he was fast. She put up her whip, not touching him, and he flew, past the post and away for a

154

second go at the racecourse. She couldn't pull him up. He was as fresh as when he had started and she couldn't get a hold on him.

They raced on; by now people from the crowd were running across the course in an effort to head him off and make him think and stop. People were yelling, shouting 'Pull up'. Which was all very well but Milkman didn't understand what that meant and had no intention of being pulled up.

Off the course and into a ditch. A filthy deep and muddy ditch which did what Elfie had been unable to do. Both she and the pony were gasping. 'Bellows to mend,' Patsy said unsympathetically as they arrived.

She felt miserable; she had let her friends down badly. Father Brown, by now arrived, told her that her instructions should have been to pull up well before the finish! The information came far too late.

She was teased all through the year, whenever she rode Milkman. 'Brought your anchor, John?' and 'There's a good stone wall half a mile back, son'. She apologised for making a fool of the pony but the priests only laughed and some time later Brother Paul laughed too, at his having been so shy on his first exposure to these sophisticated worldly racing people!

Milkman never did prove easy to pull up and would have been a great horse if only they had run races five times as long. He was a stayer, a distance pony; and races weren't for the kind of distance he needed. He'd have made a great long distance horse. For all that his difficulties made him memorable long after other horses were forgotten.

Chapter 21

Wild horses. Mild horses. Mad horses. Bad horses. Horses
that were pleasure all the way through. Horses to sell; horses
to school; horses to ride; horses to jump. Horses for hacking
and horses for hunting. Ponies for children; horses for
tradesmen; for milkfloats and for farm carts. Horses for
showing.

Rough horses; tough horses; shaggy horses; horses to
nurse; to groom; to clip; foals afraid of humans; afraid of
the blacksmith; horses that came in one day and were sold
the next; horses that stayed, unsellable until they had been
gentled and made.

Kipling's words came back so often: 'some are steady and
some will plunge'. Elfie learned to assess a horse fast; often
she saw it for the first time at the racecourse and had only
minutes to find out how it would run. She was now freelancing and building up her own tiny bank balance, hoping
not only for her own horse, but one day to run her own riding
school as she loved teaching others how to ride.

It was easier to be John Graham. Polly had to fend off men
and there were those that thought a stable girl could have
few morals and was easy game. She hadn't handled tough
horses for nothing. Nobody came back for a second lesson.
At home she was chaperoned by so many people that there
was no problem at all.

Often sitting with the family at dinner, not really listening
to their talk, she thought back over the day. One incident she
treasured with private amusement, when the family were
exceptionally tiresome.

She had spent a whole night alone in a stable with a man!
And if they had seen the man!

He was a wild character, a man who never settled

156

anywhere. He was known to everyone as 'The Missing Link'. He was an incredible man who might have been fifty or might have been a hundred; unshaven, wild-haired, his clothes as ragged as those of any tramp, with tremendously long arms, he was a wizard with wild horses. When a really bad one came in they sent for 'The Link'.

Always in afteryears when Elfie found herself dealing with a horse that huddled wild-eyed and snorting in a corner and lashed out at anyone who came near, she remembered that night.

The horse was a nice light hunter, 15.3 hands; a pretty mare with a good head that was well set on. She was terrified. Elfie wondered who had mishandled her and reduced her to a shivering animal that hated men and women alike. There was no trust in her. Only fear.

The Link had been so often that his routine was well-known. He covered the box windows with sacking. He put his flask and his butties, without which he was never seen, in the manger and then was locked in. He stayed all night, or all day. Nobody else was allowed near the animal at all.

He usually asked to be released at a set time, as if he knew to the minute just how long it would take. At the time specified Elfie knocked on the door. Silence meant 'go away, leave me alone'. A grunt meant 'Unlock, bring a cup of tea and you're welcome'.

The results were always the same. The tea was taken in and the Link would be sitting on the horse, no headcollar, no other trappings; sitting bareback with his arms folded. The horse would be standing, head down, never moving until he kicked with his heels and drove it across the box. A slap on the neck to turn it and then a gentle walk. Bring saddle and bridle. Big ones. He'd slide off, the horse still not moving, then give it a few crusts from his pack, pat it and put the bridle on. The watchers were always impressed; it looked as if the horse had been handled in this way hundreds of times before, yet up to then it had been unmanageable; no chance of touching it, let alone putting on saddle and bridle.

157

Sometimes there would be a shy, and the Link would stand and croon, murmuring unintelligible words. He might be using endearments, he might be swearing, but his voice was a soft gentle soothing reassuring sound, not much above a whisper.

Next the saddle went on and Elfie who always watched this procedure with fascination wanting to know how he did it, offered, invariably, to hold the horse. And was invariably refused. The bridle was adjusted to fit, the horse still accepting the human touch.

The saddle went on, the Link putting his arm through the rein, slapping the horse gently several times, and then gently, gently, the saddle was lowered into place, round to the other side, adjust the girths, back to the near side and slowly, slowly, girth up, as in every breaking. This part was not new to Elfie. Every movement was deliberate, and silent except for that soft murmur.

Sometimes there was tenseness and the white of a frightened eye, but the girth was done up in seconds, swiftly, surely, without fuss. Bring the horse into the light and up Link would go like a monkey. Landing feather soft, swifter moving than any jockey Elfie had ever seen and by then she had seen plenty. Then ease the horse round the yard, standing to let it look about, get used to its surroundings, with never a buck or a shy or a rear. Nothing.

Time and again as Elfie got to know him better she asked if she could stay with him. 'Please, Mr Link.' She knew he liked being called mister. Even if his name wasn't Link. She was never sure of that.

'No. I does it alone.'

She pleaded, but he always put her off. It would be hours. She'd be bored. There was nothing to see.

The day that the mare came in he looked at her. 'You still want to come?'

She couldn't believe it. Did he mean it? Yes, he did. He wouldn't let anyone else in, but she'd got 'it' he reckoned — and she knew he didn't mean sex appeal. She had a way with horses. 'No rugs,' he growled. 'I know it's cold, but no rugs.

158

Just clobber up. It's going to be a long night and you won't be getting any sleep, I can tell you.'

She put on all the clothes she could find, took spare jerseys and jacket, and went into the box sweating. There were two trusses of straw, one under the manger with Link's own clobber on it and the other went up against the door and they were locked in. Elfie could just make out shapes in the dark.

The mare looked scared and Elfie, ordered to crouch motionless, was also scared. The box seemed to shrink and the mare to grow bigger and more menacing. She wanted to watch the old man; she was sure he doped the horses. But he never moved. He sat on his truss of straw and he crooned; endlessly, monotonously, on and on, saying anything that came into his head. 'There's my beauty, there's a lovely girl, not scared are you, it's going to be a long night my pretty, there's a girl.' A soft under-his-breath endless sing-song.

Elfie sat by the manger, cold, curious and sleepy herself now, the voice lulling her as well as the mare. Hours seemed to pass and the old man, without seeming to make any movement, held out wisps of hay to the horse.

She watched him, but made no move. About half an hour later she stretched out her neck and snatched at the hay. She took a step towards him, regretted it and backed off fast. The straw rustled under her hooves. Outside the stable other people went on with their normal business. At home the family slept. Here there was only the frightened mare, the extraordinary old man and Elfie, wondering how he worked his miracles.

The hay was offered again.

The mare plucked up her courage and took it again.

The soft croon continued and Elfie dozed off. She woke with a start, at first wondering where on earth she was and then said 'Link' in a loud whisper.

He answered her in his croon but his words didn't fit the croon. 'Keep still can't you?'

She kept still. She ached with cramp and her hands and feet were frozen. Link rose from the hay, flowing to his feet

159

as if he were boneless, and slowly, still crooning, came across to Elfie, and somehow without appearing to move at all poured coffee and gave her a sandwich. She realised now that the faint light came from an old bicycle lamp hidden behind the truss of straw.

Link crouched beside her, as she warmed her hands on the mug and ate his butty. He went on crooning but now he was telling Elfie about other nights and other horses; horses far wilder than this one; he wouldn't have had her in with one of those. This was just scared; been badly used, maybe abused, and now she had to learn to trust mankind.

He forecast exactly how she would behave. The mare was relaxing; his soft voice was easing her; she was becoming inquisitive and was getting used to their smell. Both handled so many other horses that to her they smelled of horses and were not alien as someone who had nothing to do with horses would have been.

Link told Elfie to take off her jacket and gave her some bale twine.

'Pull it through the ring over there and tie it tight. Mind you move gently.'

She did as she was told and then returned to her place, leaving the jacket tied through the ring.

Link went on crooning. The mare had watched Elfie curiously and after a few minutes went to see what she had been doing. She sniffed the jacket, neck outstretched and then nibbled it. Elfie had visions of being jacketless next day. The mare returned to it curiously time and again. At last she left it.

'Put it on again,' Link said. Elfie was very glad to do so. She was cold.

The clobber that Link carried everywhere with him contained a bag of oats. Elfie wondered what else he was going to produce, like a conjuror, from the pack.

The croon went on but this time was different. 'Fill yer pockets with oats and then talk very quietly, same tone as me, and walk up to her. If she shies or whips round don't take no notice. Reckon she won't kick. Just keep on talking all the

160

time, and go bold and slow. Don't move quickly and don't dither. Let her smell it.'

Elfie held out a handful of oats.

The mare snorted and blew and smelled at it and most of it ended in the bedding. Elfie tried again, a tongue came out and licked her hand. Link turned the bicycle lamp away and sat, reading a newspaper that had mysteriously materialised out of the pack.

'Get on,' his crooning voice said. 'Or she'll get bored wi' ye.'

Elfie produced another handful from her pocket. The mare was now relaxed and came sniffing for more. She fed, and presently Elfie was able to put a hand on her neck. From behind the concealing truss on which Link sat came a bucket with oats at the bottom

'Hold her,' he said, 'and handle her as far as you can.'

'What do I hold her with?' Elfie asked. They were now able to use slightly more normal tones without the mare showing signs of panic.

'The bloody handle, of course,' Link said and at that point Elfie realised that some of his more odd turns of phrase were due to the fact that he spoke of inanimate objects as 'she' and 'he' as well as those that were alive. It explained some of her misunderstandings with him in the past.

Elfie did as she was told.

'Now get yer 'ands by her eyes and ears.' This wasn't so easy. The mare's eyes and ears were way up above Elfie's own head.

At last the mare lowered her head and Elfie fondled her till her arms ached. She was wary, but seemed quiet enough.

Link yawned. 'Carry on 'andling 'er while I get me forty winks,' he said, and rolled himself in the straw.

Within a very short time he was awake again.

'Take yer jacket off and roll it up.' Elfie obeyed. 'Now stroke her neck, withers and back, then wipe 'er wid yer jacket; then put it on her back.'

Elfie moved, but was too clumsy. The mare shied away.

'Get after 'er. Yer don't give up.'

161

Back to the mare's side, do as she was told and no bother.

'Get her back against the wall and take the hay truss over.'

The mare backed but stood watching anxiously, ears flicking, very wary.

'Get on to the truss, lean across her and play with her till I get to her.'

Elfie did as she was told and earned a reprimand.

'You've stopped talking. You may have "it" orlright but it's no good on its own. You must talk.'

She went on talking, in the dim-lit stable well into the small hours. It was hard to think of things to say.

Some time later Elfie found herself ordered to sit on the mare's back, and then the mare was moving with the weight on her, shifting round the stable. It was by then so dark that Elfie could see nothing. The bicycle lamp had become exhausted and gone out. There was no reality; it felt very odd indeed.

By dawn she was encouraging the mare with a short stick and her legs round her; the mare was quiet and willing, still nervy but the feeling was wonderful.

'Nar all yer do is sit there till we're let out.'

It seemed hours. Elfie was sleepy and her arms had cramp. She was allowed to dismount once and mounted again from the offside. She was told to fold her arms and go to sleep. She did doze, on the mare's back, waking to feel her mount shifting her own weight to get more comfortable.

At last they were released and Link led the mare outside, Elfie still seated on her, a smile of triumph on his lips.

Elfie sat, seething with suppressed excitement. She dismounted and put her hand in her pocket, feeling oats; very sweet oats; very sticky oats. Quietly she asked Link what was with the oats.

'Didn't ye larn enough widout asking questions?' he asked, and winked at her. 'Yes, they was sweetened; it's only sugar, but you have to talk nice to the sugar. Ordinary won't do. I'm not telling you any more; and don't you never tell.' Link remained Elfie's friend for many years. The mare was gentled over fifty years ago. Elfie did find out later what was

162

with the sugar, but it wasn't dope. She used his methods to calm many a horse during the rest of her long life with horses.

She kept her 'taming' coat for fifty years and it helped many nervous horses.

She wasn't always successful.

Three in particular that were her responsibility were among the greatest buckjumpers that ever appeared in or out of a rodeo. Two were successes, the third put her out for the count. They were passing the council tip when the mare swerved, relaxed, and then produced the biggest series of bucks that Elfie had ever seen or felt.

She flew, high into the air, without time to do more than realise she was out of the saddle and going to land hard. She came down on the tip, which was foul-smelling and full of broken bottles.

The mare galloped off. Elfie was found by a passing lad; she was bloody and unconscious. He raced for help. The police by then had caught the mare seven miles away.

Elfie was bruised, cut, concussed and swearing in a manner that most certainly would not have met with family approval. Her unpleasant experience left her with the utmost respect for dustmen, who have to work in such filthy surroundings. She took care never to ride near a tip again.

She remembered Patsy's words: 'Mistakes are meant to learn from. And if you don't make any, then you never learn. You can't be living.'

Chapter 22

John Graham had been riding for over two years when Elfie was offered a ride for a new owner, a pork butcher. He was new not only to her but also to racing and racehorses, and he was thrilled with his acquisition. He had great hopes of a good career for the horse. He was also pleased to get this particular jockey: he had heard a lot about young John.

'It's a good horse,' he told Elfie, without any idea that she was not the boy she appeared to be.

'What's its name?'

'Dark Secret,' the butcher said.

She nicknamed the man Porky Pete — it was one way of identifying an owner.

On the day of the race she went straight to the course. She was now much more experienced, professional in both appearance and manner, very smart in her silks, turned-out as every good jockey should be. She took one look at the horse. It was Knock On. She thought of the duckpond and hoped there was no water. She asked about his mouth, remembering the problems she had had before; he had been totally unresponsive to any signal she gave him.

Porky Pete was most impressed by her comment and quite unaware that this horse had a past known to her.

'Funny you should ask,' he said. 'We had a lot of trouble in training. He was dead on one side and they told me he always ran out. We've fixed him with a pricker.'

Elfie looked at it; it was a solution they had not tried with Knock On. There was the usual ring of two layers of strong leather, with 'prickers' (bristles) on the inside and a slit in the leather for it to be fitted round the bit. On the other side was an identical ring made of plain leather. Elfie realised she would have to ride a bit canny.

164

She met an old enemy at the line-up. It was to be a day for reunions but this one was very unwelcome. There, large as ever and twice as ugly, was Wild Willie, who looked at her, grinned at her and said, 'Got yer swimsuit, Nancy?' She had become used to some of the rougher men calling her a pansy or a nancy boy or a sissy. She might be able to fool them in some ways but there she was not a tough customer at all. But by now she took most things in her stride and the gibe didn't bother her.

Willie was as big and tough and unshaven and dirty as before; he was riding a different pony, and he decided that he was going to get Elfie off, come what might. He knew she was likely to beat him; she was a frequent winner now, or if not winning, often among the first three past the post. He kept as near to her as he could, all the way, looking for opportunities. It was one of the wildest rides she'd had for a long time. He rode close, he jostled, he tried to bump her, he tried to tip her, but Knock On was big and tough and just kept going. Once the whip lashed almost in her face, but she saw it coming, ducked and rode on, determined not to be beaten by foul riding.

There was no duck pond and the pricker worked. They had passed the winning post and were riding in triumph back to Porky Pete when Willie rode up and spat at her. 'I'll get yer, yer little runt.' He came so close that she could smell his breath as he leaned towards her. She hoped, fervently, that they would never meet again.

Porky Pete was watching her and as she came towards him he suddenly yelled, 'Whoa, there.' She pulled up sharp, the saddle shot up on to the horse's neck and Elfie came off, landing on her feet, the saddle on the ground beside her. Porky Pete picked it up and stared at the girth.

It had been sliced clean through.

'Who the devil would play a dirty trick like that on me?' he asked.

'It wasn't on you, it was on me. I'm pretty certain I know who it is; I beat him once before. And he is a devil. Can't prove it; I'll just have to watch him all the time.'

Nobody could work out how it had been done. Elfie went home vowing vengeance; she'd had a bad fright and he needed a lesson. She'd never done him any harm but she knew he was a bad loser and nobody liked him.

Luckily for her conscience in after years they did not ride in the same race again, and some time later Patsy commented that some bright spark had nicked Wild Willie's stirrup leathers and he'd fallen at the gallop and broken his collar bone. Somebody else had taken revenge, probably for a similar trick. After that incident she always checked her equipment very carefully before she rode, although she was pretty sure the girth-cutting had been done with her in the saddle; a very quick deft trick while he distracted her as he swore. She never met Knock On again either and was rather sorry; he had done her proud.

One of her unfavourite owners was a real trickster, always up to something. He was not easy to ride for and he had to be obeyed to the letter; he had a very nasty turn of temper and a very powerful tongue. Often his instructions seemed anything but honest. One of his ponies had three different names in one season. He was turned out rough and scruffy at one meeting: bridle and saddle had seen vastly better days and were in need of repair, although quite safe. At another he was beautifully groomed and plaited, with legs kept bandaged all the time, looking like a Thoroughbred, with highly expensive tack to match. Even the horsebox matched. At the third he was clipped-out, hogged and his tail was shortened to above his hocks. Elfie had to prepare him according to instructions and although she was responsible for his appearance each time, even she was amazed at how different he looked.

She had to ride him differently each time, but always out to win. The owner wanted long odds, which was the object of the game — had the pony been known as a winner the bookies would have made sure that no one made much on him. As an unknown they might well be at 100-1. John Graham was learning all the time and a lot of the things he learned were rather odd. It was a very liberal education for a girl with her family background.

That particular pony was very fast and kept very fit, but he was very hard to hold and not amenable to his rider's ideas. He was scatterbrained and always jumped straight into a gallop and kept up the pace, so that she needed to try and pull out more than he had at times at the finish as he'd gone too fast for his own good. The more steady runners still had something left in reserve. He would never hold back or be placed where she wanted him, lying well back till it was time to make the pace. If she could have ridden him as she wanted he would have flown at the end; as it was he exhausted himself by his efforts.

Sometimes as a result he packed in at the end of race. At others he would win easily, but there was no way he could ever be asked to make more effort if he did not choose. He would slow down, or pull out, and set his jaw and Elfie would pass the post shoulders and neck first.

At one meeting he started his go-slow early and she battled with her whip and spurs and arms to try and straighten him out. He pulled himself together, pushed ahead and seemed to be giving his best when, with the winning post only a hundred yards away he set his head at an angle again, his jaw iron hard. But he was galloping well.

Elfie was neck and neck with one of the wild boys. She was using her whip to try and keep the pony straight; the winning post was only a couple of furlongs away. Then the rider next to her lashed his whip straight across her face. Blinded by tears of pain, she brought up her whip in self-defence, but she couldn't see. She tried desperately to stay in the saddle as she had no idea where the horse was going or where the winning post now was. She couldn't stop the pouring tears and her face hurt abominably. She hadn't the least idea what happened next; she was aware of a terrific surge of acceleration from her startled horse, then a heavy crash and she lay there, winded, knowing she and the pony were both on the floor. She could see the winning post behind them.

The pony's owner was furious. He had seen what had

happened. He helped her up and they soothed the pony. The judges had a tricky decision; Elfie had skidded through the finish on the ground, her leg trapped under the pony, could she be the winner? She was — though she wondered afterwards if her owner's threatening behaviour had influenced the judges as he was blazing mad at the way his jockey had been treated. She had never allowed that owner to learn her secret but there was another there who did know and was concerned: his girl rider was taking some pretty hefty knocks and although he could shelter her up to a point, he couldn't ride with her and keep off the roughs.

She was covered in mud and turf but miraculously unhurt and rode in the next race still filthy, with split breeches and a sleeve missing.

A few days later she did have a far worse fright. She was travelling in a box without anyone from the yard and one of the other lads travelling was Joey Dodd, a big rough lad with the meanest riding habits of anyone she knew. They tumbled out, stiff after the long journey. Time to stretch their legs before unloading and then to prepare the ponies.

Elfie solved the changing problem by wearing her racing silks under her everyday grey flannels and jersey; all she had to do was strip those off and she was ready. The colours were always either very good silks or a coloured jersey to suit the owner, and silk caps, but no protective headgear. She was soon ready.

She wasn't too popular with some of the lads; for one thing she won or was placed too often. One or two were decent, thinking her a schoolboy in need of protection, but the others called her Titch or Fleabite, or less savoury names and today Joey was determined to bully all he could. Most of the teasing was harmless, but Joey was malicious and she took a lot of extra stick because she wouldn't match their swearing. She had a posh accent and was a delicate-looking type without their range of vocabulary.

Permanent waves had just become fashionable and she had had her short hair set in tight curls all over her head. She suddenly realised that when she took off her cap there would be comment. It was the first time her dual personality had really conflicted at the races. The cap came off and there was a roar of laughter. Someone rumpled her hair and said she was a real little sissy-boy and looked more like a girl, a statement that suddenly worried her considerably. Joey looked at her and laughed.

'Proper little fancy man, isn't he? What do you bet he has to sit down to pee?'

There was another roar of laughter and as they started off for the racecourse Joey turned to her and said, 'Get in the box, you, and pee with the others.'

She didn't need to and didn't want to but she was lifted by the scruff of the neck and thrown in to the box where two other lads were relieving themselves.

They watched her. She had a considerable problem now; she had always managed to avoid it before by timing her exits cleverly and disappearing behind trees.

She had no idea what to do so she turned her back, undid her fly, straddled her legs and hoped they would not notice that nothing whatever was happening. Fortunately, they were far too busy themselves and made enough noise for three people, so that they did not realise there was no sound from her. Also they were swopping jokes. She buttoned up and turned. Then knocked on the door to be let out. Joey met her with another roar of laughter, grabbed her and tried to pull off her pants. She kicked, hard, and managed to avoid him, and two of the others, tired of the bullying, came to her rescue, still unaware of the real reason for her obvious distress.

'Let the kid alone, can't you?' Joey, thwarted, treated her to a stream of abuse using words she hadn't heard before and didn't understand. She was used to the men swearing, but this was something else and even the other lads found his foul language distasteful and left him to it.

She was now really frightened, especially as they were to ride in the same race and she was expected to win. She was also afraid that succumbing to the temptation to have her hair curled had given Joey a clue as to her sex; and that he

169

intended to find out for himself. She wasn't going to travel home with them whatever happened, although she had no idea how she could avoid it. She remembered the last time she had ridden against Joey. He had cornered her before the start and threatened to beat her up if her pony won. She knew he had done it to others and she had despised them for succumbing, but faced with violence that she could not return she too had succumbed, too frightened to risk him carrying out his threats. She had not dared to win and when she saw that she might she eased up on her pony and let Joey have his way.

She had been unhappy ever since. She had liked her owner and felt she had let him down badly. Today she was again riding for a good owner who played very straight and she didn't want to let him down. But if she went home in that horsebox and had won, it was going to cost her dearly; and it might be the end of her racing career if the men found out she was a woman. The thought of the long journey back with Joey made her feel sick.

The race was as frightening as she had expected. Joey clung beside her all the way; she was too aware of him but this time she would win if the pony had it in him and she set out to ride hellbent, using all her skill to get to the post. She did her best to forget Joey, although it was difficult. The pony was a flier and was lengths ahead at the finish, an easy winner. Joey took it as badly as she expected, and promised that she wouldn't be able to walk when she got out of the box at the end of the journey. He'd see to that. The only consolation was that he hadn't realised John was a girl and that his taunts were in fact the absolute truth. It was quite obvious he thought that John Graham was a rather wet lad from a posh home, unable to stand up for himself.

'I'll teach you not to come slumming, you little fop,' he said.

The box had been driven by her owner. He was with Father Denny, who was also at the meeting as 'John' was to ride their pony later in the afternoon. She told them that Joey had cut up rough at losing and told them of his threats before the race. She couldn't travel in the box. He was a big man and strong and a bully and she was terrified of him. She hoped they wouldn't think her a coward and a pansy boy, but she no longer cared: she couldn't face Joey and the journey home in the closed-in box, entirely at his mercy. The others couldn't stand up to him either. It had taken all the pleasure out of winning.

Her owner was driving the box with his brother as a passenger, but the brother was a cripple and couldn't travel in the rear so Elfie would have to travel squashed on to the gearbox. She didn't care. At least she would be safe.

Only they were due, as always, to celebrate with a stop at the pub on the way home. Joey half-drunk was much worse than Joey sober and they would all be in the pub; they couldn't lock him in the box; and she couldn't stay there alone because he might come out and find her.

Father Denny found a way out for her: he offered to take her home in his little Austin Seven. She could have her evening meal with the priests and then go on home afterwards. It would solve everything. The priest had been watching with some interest during the afternoon and he had half guessed at the situation. He had no idea that the jockey they liked so much was a girl but it was obvious to anyone that John was no match for the tough lads that loved to use their physical strength and make life a misery for anyone less strong than they were. He had seen Joey's face when he lost and he had taken care, without Elfie even realising it, to see that she wasn't at any time alone that afternoon. He might be a priest but he was a big tough Irishman and he had a sharp tongue. She rode again, later that afternoon, for Father Denny, this time in a race without Joey. She was tired out with the strain of riding and the strain of fear by the time they left for home, and she was thankful to sit quietly, saying nothing, and sleep a little on the drive. She woke feeling the time had come to reveal the truth; she simply dared not risk another ride with Joey in a horsebox. She did wish more than ever that she had been born a boy. It was so stupid to ban occupations to girls.

171

It wasn't the first time she had been to a meal at the Presbytery. She knew the priests well and also their Scottish housekeeper, Mrs McPhee. John Graham was supposed to be a Scot, so the housekeeper had a very soft spot for the lad. Not one of those rough types at all; very suitable for the good fathers. She wasn't sure that owning a racehorse went with priesthood but if they had to race then this lad was ideal for them. A nice refined polite boy with good manners. Elfie always remembered to raise her cap when she was a boy and met ladies.

The kitchen was warm and friendly, with a good fire blazing and the cat lying on the rug. Mrs McPhee had a cup of tea for her, to revive her before she washed. The meal wasn't ready and, although the housekeeper didn't quite approve of racing, she wanted to hear how the fathers' pony had run.

'I don't know what to do,' Elfie said, suddenly sure the story had to come out and not at all sure how to begin.

'About what? Tell me,' the housekeeper said, aware as she looked at the lad that there was a very worrying problem; he looked half sick to death and roused all her motherly instincts.

'I'm not John Graham,' she said.

'Don't be daft, lad. Who else can you be? We've known you for years.' She wondered if the horse had kicked him on the head and addled his wits.

'I'm Elspeth Pollok; I worked for Patsy; he started me riding as a boy. When I left him I thought it would be fun to go on freelancing as John Graham and it is, often; but now I'm scared.'

Mrs McPhee stared at her.

'Yes. Now I know I can see you're a lass and not a lad. You'd better tell me all about it.'

Elfie told her. She didn't realise she was actually telling a great deal more than she intended, so the housekeeper got a vivid picture of the child who had longed for movement; of the family that so scorned her; and of the difficulty of leading even her normal life without adding to the problems

172

of riding as a boy in a man's world and a very rough world at that.

'Landsakes,' was all she could think of to say.

'Please tell Father Denny for me,' Elfie said.

'You're a Scots lassie and they don't run away; tell him yourself now,' Mrs McPhee said. 'The fathers are used to confessions; they'll have heard plenty worse. It's best to do it yourself and they'll respect you for it if you do tell them and not leave it to me.'

The room where they ate was always friendly, the fire blazing in the grate, the brass irons polished till they shone; the food plentiful and well cooked. Elfie sat, eating supper, a spoonful of whisky in her tea, as they could see she was exhausted. They didn't bother her with much talk. Racing was a gruelling business and they knew their jockey would be tired.

She sat enjoying the peace of the room, so different from the strained meals at home and the constant family disapproval. The priests were at ease with one another; they joked and talked and discussed the future of their ponies and heard about the racing that afternoon and also about Elfie's problem with Joey. She didn't know quite how to begin, but a visitor came, a young man who wanted to see two of the priests so that she was left alone with Father Denny.

Firelight was flickering on the fire irons and fender and Elfie kept her eyes on the glittering brass.

'Father, I've got a confession. I'm in trouble.' He looked at her, startled, but said, 'Tell me, my boy' and listened quietly as she went right back to the beginning for the second time that night.

'Holy Mother of God!'

He got up and patted her on the head. He yelled for Father Paul and Father Joseph and for Mrs McPhee and for whisky and when they all came, began to speak and instead started to laugh. He laughed till he had to hold his sides and tears ran down his face. When at last he could control himself he grinned at them and said, 'Now wait for the best story any of ye have heard in years!'

By the time it was told everyone was laughing, even Elfie.

'Ah, well I'd heard rumours and I have wondered,' Father Joseph said. 'But I couldn't go up to her and ask her could I now? I didn't believe it at first and then I decided to say nothing; it could be just spiteful gossip because our lad was a little bit unusual; too gentle for a lad, and he makes a better girl. And a different background to most of them. They don't like posh accents. Or being beaten.'

'I never guessed,' Father Denny said, and both Mrs McPhee and Father Joseph agreed she had done well; they had never even considered her as a girl, although now they knew, it was obvious.

'Does it mean I can't ride for you any more?' Elfie asked.

'Not a bit of it; but we'll have to take a great deal more care of you and look after you a lot better. You make a much better girl than you do a funny wee lad to be quite honest. And now for what Mrs McPhee would call a wee dram and then off home with you.'

From then on there was a conspiracy of owners to keep her from coming up against the rough types more than was necessary. She remained John to everyone, including the priests and their housekeeper, and none of the other riders knew, but it was soon a very-well-kept secret among the owners that their gem of a jockey was actually a girl. They valued her winning too much to ever let on, and she began to enjoy the role of John Graham as she had not before, and be happy that she had no secrets from the men who mattered to her, as she wanted very much to go on racing. Nothing in life could ever replace that thrill, or the knowledge of a well-run race and a well-deserved win.

Chapter 23

Life at work was a great deal easier and happier once the owners realised their jockey was a girl. They were very proud of her, taking an amused proprietorial interest, especially as she so often beat the men at a skill that was considered impossible for a woman.

She was used to keeping her own counsel. It had never done to talk about her work at home, except to Madeline. It was always easier to work late and arrive at an impossible hour for family dinner. She enjoyed the conspiratorial suppers eaten off a well-scrubbed table in the big warm kitchen, the coal fire blazing. It was far more comfortable than in the prim and remarkably chilly family dining-room.

She was too busy to worry overmuch about the family and their attitude. Her days were so full with all the work, with training, with schooling, with lessons, with demonstrating the paces of a horse that was for sale, that by evening she was physically and mentally too jaded to even want company.

She could at times relax with the priests and Mrs McPhee, enjoying a meal after a well-run race; and there was always the race to discuss with the owner she had been riding for. Next time should she ride the same, or perhaps see if the pony needed different treatment?

She thought about it all the time; discussed it with Patsy. Fancy likes to be out in front, but there's nothing in her at the finish. Maybe a different bit would suit Father Paul's pony? That new pony's topheavy, all head and is a beast to ride — can we school her a bit and get that head up? That new colt kicks; watch him. And the piebald pony shies at shadows; need to be careful when she's being ridden by an inexperienced rider. Don't give her to Mrs Tomlinson; she's very nervous.

Horses might be ill, go lame, need treatment or special feeding or a routine to get them fit. Horses came in for them to care for as the owners didn't know how; horses with Monday morning sickness; overfed ponies with laminitis. There were ponies bought as show hopes with no spark in them; horses bought for jumping that couldn't jump a piece of string in the grass; horses bought for breeding that appeared to be barren.

It was a totally different world to that inhabited by the family. They might have lived in different planets for all that they understood one another.

It was a lonely world in some ways, as it was obviously impossible to make friends among the other jockeys; they were all male. But sometimes she did make tentative friendships with some of the girls of her own age who came to learn to ride.

She was not popular with the horse people when it came to competition: she often beat them and nobody likes to lose. But she needed a friend, someone she could laugh with, chat with, share a few secrets with, and her triumphs. Not to brag, but just to talk. She met someone who seemed to understand and trusted her with her greatest secret and told her about John Graham.

Elfie was not a jealous person; she had known too much misery and pain in her own life and she always insisted that any disabled child they knew was allowed to ride at the yard free. She knew how it felt to be unable to do as others did, unable to walk or ride, and she could sympathise with the stutterers and the pathologically shy and handle them as she handled an unhappy pony; with understanding, patience and skill.

She made mistakes and knew she made them, but never made the same mistake twice. She raced often; not always winning, but winning often enough to want to share the thrill with her new friend; trying to make her see the excitement, and the sheer pleasure and satisfaction that came from doing any job well; this was just another part of her daily work and one that would have been taken for granted if she had been a man.

She had chosen her friend unwisely. There was Elfie having all the fun; doing things other women couldn't do; riding round the country, enjoying a full, active life that seemed a riot of excitement to a girl who spent her days in routine jobs; no thrills, no spills, no racing, no winning. No triumphs anywhere, ever. The friend convinced herself that it was wrong; Elfie was leading a very wicked life and her Family Ought To Know. Then the fun would end.

Elfie was used to the racecourse treachery but not to treachery in her personal life. She enjoyed having one person in her own circle to talk to and trust.

She had no idea that anything was wrong, beyond the normal disapproval of her stable work.

She came home fairly early after a very busy day.

Unusually, Madeline was waiting at the door, having been watching for Elfie's arrival.

'Quick,' she said. 'Your red velveteen and your silk stockings are on the bed; I've lit the gasfire. Go and have a bath and for goodness sake wash your hair and dry it by the fire. You've got half an hour.'

'What's so important?' Elfie asked, puzzled. She had never been met like this before and could think of nothing in the family's life to deserve it. There was no anniversary she had forgotten; no birthday. An impending engagement? She was mystified.

'They know what you've been doing. Somebody's thought it her duty to tell them. Now hurry. There's trouble; bad trouble.'

Elfie ran upstairs. She washed her hair as she bathed, and rubbed it dry by the gasfire, running a comb through and through it, wishing it wasn't always so soft and fine and flyaway; it was pestilential hair. Other people had lovely hair: soft shining blonde curls, or thick blue-black tresses that lay smooth and sleek. Her hair always annoyed her. It was better to concentrate on her hair than on the ordeal ahead; to dress meticulously, and look at herself in the mirror; no longer Polly the stable girl, but Mr Ted's little princess. She remembered her birthday night and wished her father was still alive. He would have understood. It was her most frequent wish; he had left her so alone.

Madeline slipped into the room, took the comb and sleeked the babysoft hair. She looked at Elfie critically. 'Time to go down,' she said.

Elfie wanted to run, back to the yard, back to sanctuary. The family were scathing enough about working with horses, she couldn't even imagine what they would say about racing. She hated the family rows; they left her with knotted muscles, feeling sick, her hands and teeth clenched in misery and completely unable ever to put her own viewpoint; or if she tried to she was talked down.

She realised as soon as she walked into the room that this was going to be not a row but an explosion. They were ranged against her, cold faces looking at her. Her mother, her eldest brother, the most important uncle and aunt, and added to them was one of the directors of the family firm.

Elfie stood in the doorway, looking for an empty seat.

There wasn't one.

She had no intention of standing there like a schoolgirl in front of her teachers, so she walked to the windowsill and sat on that; it was broad and low and they often used it as a seat.

It wasn't as bad as she had expected. It was far, far worse.

The angry words were launched at her. She had let the family down enough by working with those common men in a stable with horses; but this ... no one could bring themselves to express what they thought; it was unspeakable, it was unthinkable, it was indiscreet, it was compromising, it was degrading. It was the most disgusting behaviour they had ever heard of; mixing with scum and vagabonds.

Driving round the country with anybody; eating meals in these terrible people's houses. She thought of the Presbytery and Mrs McPhee who was in constant attendance now that she knew 'John' was a girl, never leaving her alone with the

178

fathers at all, and of the courtesy she received from her owners.

Every time she tried to speak one of the solemn outraged voices talked her down, telling her how unspeakable she was; unfit for decent society.

'All day with horses; I think your wits have been addled,' her brother said.

Her mind was seething and absurdly into it came a couple of lines from a poem of Walter de la Mare's that she had loved: '*He is crazed with the spell of far Arabia; they have stolen his wits away.*'

She gave up trying to say anything and sat seething with misery and fury, as there was no way at all of coping with them or of getting them to understand that the world was changing. It was now 1934, not 1913.

Elspeth's mother was sitting in a big wing chair, listening but saying nothing.

Now she spoke. Just one word.

'Silence.'

The din died down.

'Elspeth, what have you got to say for yourself?'

The use of her full name showed her the extent of her mother's displeasure. It was only used in the gravest circumstances.

'I'm freelancing. Riding for different owners. They're very respectable people. It's not at all the way you imagine.'

Well, only at times and that had stopped now. She had never told others about the bullying men; only Patsy and the owner she rode for that day and the priests and they would never tell anyone else. She gave some names and addresses.

'And who is this John Graham you go about with?'

'I'm John Graham.'

They couldn't understand; her betrayer hadn't explained herself properly and they had thought Elfie spent all her time with this man. It was difficult at first to know who had informed on her; but the number of those who could was limited and although she only learned for certain sometime later that it had been the girl she thought a good friend, she

179

became wary of making any friends at all and isolated herself even more after that night.

She was not going to change her way of life to suit the family. She had learned too many skills and there was a chance in the future that she might turn them to good use.

She had to leave home. The opportunity came after Patsy had sold his yard. The new owners only wanted a riding school, and she didn't want to stay with strangers.

She spent her time freelancing for anyone who wanted her. She rode in races, plaited, clipped and schooled horses, getting the work from those who had known her at the yard and on recommendation from her owners, working at her clients' homes. She was always busy. She had less and less to do with her family.

She was becoming very well known among the horse-owning fraternity.

One day she jumped a mare for a Cheshire man. She was a good horse and she did very well indeed. On the strength of that performance and the knowledge that Miss Pollok would bring in a lot of her own clients, he offered her a job.

She was to run the riding school; break in horses, be responsible for all the livery, clipping, plaiting that came in and to live in.

To live in. A chance to leave the family and live her own kind of life? It was too good to miss. The job had been offered on the day of her competition jumping and she had not seen the place. The man was a farmer and she was shocked at his tatty yard: ill-kept horses, a nightmare of a tack room, jumbled bridles dropped anyhow, saddles, girths, stirrups, rugs, all filthy and moth-eaten or mouse-eaten.

It was crazy. It was impossible. It was a challenge. She took a week's holiday and then started.

She worked from early morning until it was too dark to see. There was plenty of straw and no one rationed it so boxes were mucked out twice every day. She whitewashed walls and mended doors; the horses were turned out into the paddock, apparently for the first time ever as they went wild, rolling off all the loose, matted hair. They were as filthy as the yard. Patsy would have had twenty fits and put on one of his best yelling acts.

It was tough, it was dirty, but she enjoyed every moment; no going home at night to strained family meals, to disapproval, to creeping in through the kitchen as if she were the disgrace they thought. She was able to do as she chose; to see her work prosper, to watch the horses begin to shine. They came into newly cleaned smart boxes and were groomed and trimmed and she felt as proud as if they were her own.

It took time and sometimes she felt as if she were in charge of the Augean stables; her only help were the hordes of willing children at weekends; prepared to muck out and clean tack, anything to be with horses. She remembered her own childhood days and the Shire stables and Nancy, and the children were always welcome. She encouraged those who were disabled to ride.

She loved giving riding lessons; they were a welcome break from hard work. So many of her old pupils came back to her, now that she had a base to teach from. She had to do all the stable work and seemed for ever to be removing her whitewash-splashed dungarees, then scrubbing herself in cold water, as her room was as primitive as the rest of the place and changing into highly polished boots, smart gaiters, breeches, jacket and bowler, so that she set an example to her pupils when giving a lesson. A scruffy instructor did not invite respect. And many of them had known her in a much more prosperous-looking yard.

Once she forgot to remove her bowler hat as she hurried back into dungarees to finish whitewashing and it was never quite the same again.

Gradually the place changed into a smart riding school. The farm midden was removed from the middle of the yard; post and rail fencing was put up and a cinder track made an exercising ground. The tack room was refurbished, with bridle and saddle racks, their owners' names above; the rugs were washed and packed in a big trunk and electric

181

light was put in and all the outside woodwork was painted.

The school prospered.

Elfie found that once the place was running smoothly some of the excitement went; the clients were pleasant and she made good friends; her employer's children were delightful, although their mother rarely appeared and she disliked her owner, who persistently reminded her of Uriah Heep. But she missed the excitement and busyness and companionship of Patsy's yard and, oddly, in a perverse way she missed her home. Her room was bare and bleak and cheerless; it was better to keep on working and polishing tack and dealing with odd jobs until bedtime. It was a cold kind of existence, and sometimes she felt she was teaching in her sleep.

'Now, Sharon, he's a lovely pony but remember he doesn't know you yet. Talk to him; let him come to you and never chase him or grab him, which is what you have just done, poor pony. He isn't naughty; he's puzzled and frightened. Look, Sharon; walk up slowly, like I do, and have you got pony nuts or polo mints today? He loves polos.'

It was so hard to make some people understand their naughty horses weren't naughty at all; just puzzled or miserable or confused or being ridden like machines; drag on the reins, race after them, yelling, and terrify them. How could she put it over better? How could she make them understand? How could she make them see as the Missing Link had made her see just what was needed to succeed with a horse?

At times irritation did take over and afterwards she would say of her pupil: 'She couldn't ride in a pram with the hood up!'

Or: 'For heaven's sake, call those hands? I've seen better sold as pigs trotters in a tripe shop.'

She couldn't bear to see a horse misused by a clumsy rider.

'Why did he shy, Miss Pollok? It's only a cat.'

'Only a cat, leaping out of the grass like that? Only a cat! But it jumped and frightened him, so soothe him. Tell him,

182

for goodness sake; he's never seen a cat before. It's all right Brownie, it's only a cat.'

Get into the horse's skin; think about those two eyes on either side of his head and what does he see? Not what we see, for sure. What does he know? Nothing that we know.

Teaching at the farm began to pall. She wanted her own school. She wanted her own horses; she wanted to be her own mistress. There was no future in running other people's stables.

At last the day came when she had her own riding school. She could develop her old skill of trick riding, which brought back a little of the thrill of the racing days; she could have her own pupils, and could run things the way she wanted.

She looked at the ramshackle yard. It was a ruin of a place, a mass of tumbledown sheds; at 'her' horses and ponies, in their stalls; they were lent or borrowed, but she was ready to start on her own; another beginning. She had built up her former employer's yard from nothing; she had done it all before; this time she was working for herself and that alone made a big difference. She saw the future; the spick and span yard; the well-kept ponies and horses belonging entirely to her; a way of earning a living. So many people had helped her; among them the man who was to be her husband in a year or so's time. She looked at the printed cards.

MISS ELFIE POLLOK'S RIDING SCHOOL
AND LIVERY STABLE

Horses for sale and hire
Children's ponies
trained for Show Ring
a Speciality
Hunting

It was a very long way indeed from Elfie in her wheel-chair, dreaming of riding.

AFTERWARDS

Elfie worked all day, every day, and half the night to get her riding school in order. Her previous employers had trained her remarkably well and within the year it became a show place. She rode still for some of her previous racing owners. She needed to earn so she showjumped, she broke horses and ponies, she rode for dealers and she began to show children's ponies, not realising that yet again she was laying a foundation for the future. She opened her riding school in 1935. It was to remain part of her working life right up to the late 1970s when she retired.

She began to buy in ponies, breaking them and teaching them good manners, preparing them for a future as a child's ride and then selling them. She bought ponies very cheaply, but good food and good training made those she produced so sought-after that they commanded very high prices. She sold, mostly, privately, but those not good enough for the show ring went to auction in Wrexham. Even there, her ponies were the most sought-after.

She had been running the riding school for four years when she married. 1939 was a bad year for Britain and those who remember it remember too the four years of total hardship that followed the outbreak of war. Her husband was a farmer and therefore in a reserved occupation; farms were short-handed, run with as few people as possible — perhaps if the farmer was lucky, a landgirl or two. Elfie and her husband, as all young people do, needed money. Elfie kept on the riding stables and in her spare time also worked on the farm.

There were not enough hours in the day. Animals can never be left unfed; stables need cleaning out and horses had to be groomed and exercised. She gave up racing (that was easy as nothing went on during the war) and she had been trick riding which brought in money for charity and she worked, devotedly, for the Red Cross and other wartime charities, but she became pregnant in 1940 and, although she continued to work and to ride, trick riding had to be abandoned as likely to damage the baby.

The war affected everybody; only those in special occupations could have petrol coupons; cars were commandeered and so, Elfie discovered, were good horses. All her hunters went; the compensation was very little and they couldn't be replaced.

She had to use her wits. Pony traps began to replace cars so she broke trap ponies; plough horses began to replace tractors and she broke horses for the plough. She broke Thoroughbreds and point-to-pointers; and she took on more and more harness work. To add to her problems an all-wise government billeted two munition workers on her. They took everything in their stride, but she fought her own war with food shortages for the horses, although her work with breaking meant she could get rations for them. She now had to learn to cook.

She had, by 1944, three daughters; there was also her work on the farm and her work in the stables; she had babies and her husband to care for and the munition workers to feed; Canadians, Polish and American soldiers and airmen came to ride. The work was unremitting; it was exhausting; it was endless and the children had to be brought up as well.

Midnight could well find her still working in the stables, with tack to clean and the horses done up at night and people turning up for jumping now that racing had stopped. She ran small horse shows to raise money for charity; she worked in spite of air raids and coped with shortages of human food as well as horse food.

Many people, now famous, came to ride in the years that followed: Charlie Kunt, Jack Hulbert, Karl Brossin (remembered with affection because he always brought her orchids when he came to hire a horse). Actors and actresses from the Liverpool theatre came out for relaxation. One name particularly remembered was that of Tom Wall. Years later a horse he owned named April the Fifth was running in the Grand National. Elfie, who rarely betted, backed it for old times' sake, and won a good sum of money on it.

Her first marriage ended and she went to live in Hoylake, where she started a riding school at West Kirkby on Meol's Drive. She had a contract with the nearby boys' school that helped tremendously as she had the three girls to bring up on her own.

Later she moved back to Grange Hill stables and sold the school at West Kirkby to Sheila Algeo who had worked for her for a very long time, had left to play her part in the war, and who brought back with her Geoffrey Montgomery. They married and now run a very successful stables in Gloucestershire.

Then she met Bill Bryce-Smith and with him came to Anglesey where from 1947-59 they ran a successful market gardening business. But she couldn't give up horses; she showed ponies all over Britain and broke in the children's ponies; she longed to get back to working with horses all the time. Her own children rode and jumped and showed ponies for her.

Bill's health was bad and in 1959 it broke down completely. Elfie couldn't manage the market garden on her own and she now had an invalid to care for as well. The only thing she could do well was work with horses. And then Trefor came on the market. But money was tight and Elfie did not know how she could afford the place.

By now the family were very proud of her; life had changed completely in that respect. Elspeth Bryce-Smith was now a considerable personality in the horse world. Her mother had felt it a pity that Bill and the market garden had diverted Elfie from what she knew best. She had backed her daughter long ago when she took her first job at the stables; now she became a major support, both financially and as a morale booster, providing the money to buy Trefor, and making the idea become a reality. Trefor had potential; there was a dilapidated house and neglected grounds; and nowhere at all for horses. Elfie's life had become very difficult as she was torn in two directions, but Bill's breakdown convinced her that this was the only way she could go; she had no experience of any other way of life.

She had no room at the nursery to expand and in 1959 had a number of ponies booked in for residence; Emrys and Derek Gethrins from Montgomeryshire had booked in their ponies and so had the De Villes and the Payne Evans' daughter Susan. There was no way she could fulfill those obligations and work the gardens without a man to help her.

Trefor proved to be Bill's salvation. He hated horses (which was why Elfie had tried to become a market gardener) but he loved working with his hands, and when he came out of hospital after a long spell of illness he began to improve the place. He not only spent much of his time doing carpentry but also drove the horseboxes to shows. Without his help many of the Trefor events would have been far more taxing, as he took on a great deal of work when he was well. The trouble that plagued him was never to get better, only worse, but he managed for much of the time to overcome his difficulties and work alongside his wife, backing her in every way. Her eldest daughter, Tilda, was now her partner and a major influence. Elfie could never had managed without her.

I rode at Trefor for the first time in 1962. I found it hard to believe that they had moved into a broken-down place only two years before as by then they had built stables (which they did themselves) and the place was full of horses. It was a busy place with several girls helping (I never did sort out Elfie's daughters then) and Bob Wilkinson had come back into her life as Riding Master. His wife and daughters had come to Anglesey with him and they had a cottage nearby.

He had worked in the Royal Mews and had fascinating stories about the Windsor Greys. He also had a story about the tiny boy who rode round the Mews on his tricycle making aeroplane noises; it had been some time before he realised it was Prince Charles.

Trefor grew; hundreds of people all over the country will

remember the residential courses; the gymkhanas, and the jumping; the shows that were held there; the ponies that Elfie showed so successfully still, and that were in such high demand.

Most of the horse people I meet have a story to tell about Elfie; how when they had given up hope for a horse she gave them a herbal treatment that worked when the vet had failed; the foals she helped into the world; the horses she gentled; the emergencies she dealt with.

She made another dream come true, as when she went to Trefor she started classes for disabled riders. Now everyone knows of Riding for the Disabled, but then it was in its infancy. Riders came to her free; and if they could benefit from being taught they were, and dozens of people who had only known an existence dependent on others for help knew for the first time the wonderful freedom that came from being able to direct their own horse.

Now she has only memories; memories of so many people, far too many to mention here; grateful memories of all those who backed her, who helped her, who gave her support in so many ways; memories that are her own, seen through her eyes. I wrote her story from her diaries; others may not have seen events as she saw them. How could they? They were onlookers, not knowing what she was thinking or how she was feeling. It is a very personal viewpoint; her own viewpoint; possibly she felt more disapproval than the family intended; possibly she was oversensitive in many ways; no one can ever know, in its entirety, how it feels to be someone else; everyone is so individual. But the sensitive lonely child who dreamed of horses made her dreams come true.

The little girl in the wheelchair had realised all her dreams; now nearly seventy years later her only canters are once more in the clouds; but with what memories! She still has contact with horses as her grandchildren ride; and alone by the fire at night, she can savour the memories of still nights and the patient beasts and know too, as the letters come through her door, that thanks to her there are hundreds of people who remember hours of pleasure that they enjoyed because of her unremitting work.

She remembers them; too many to mention but few have been forgotten; her people, who rode her horses; and who will remember her, and know that although they haven't been mentioned in her story, they all had their place in her life.

'What do you remember best of your life with horses?' I asked her.

The answer came immediately.

'Evening stables. Last thing at night, before I went to bed, I always went to look at the horses. They stood quietly, and greeted me: hay in the haynets, and clean bedding; the lovely smell of a well-cared-for horse; the heads watching me; the silence, except for the rustle in the straw. All's well at the end of the day. Only those who live with horses can ever know what tremendous satisfaction that last look round gives you.'

I could see her, alone, when the moon was high and the owls calling in the woods round Trefor, walking down for the last long look; could see the heads and the watching eyes, and savour the peace that comes when you can go to bed knowing that the job has been done and well done, and all is well with your charges.